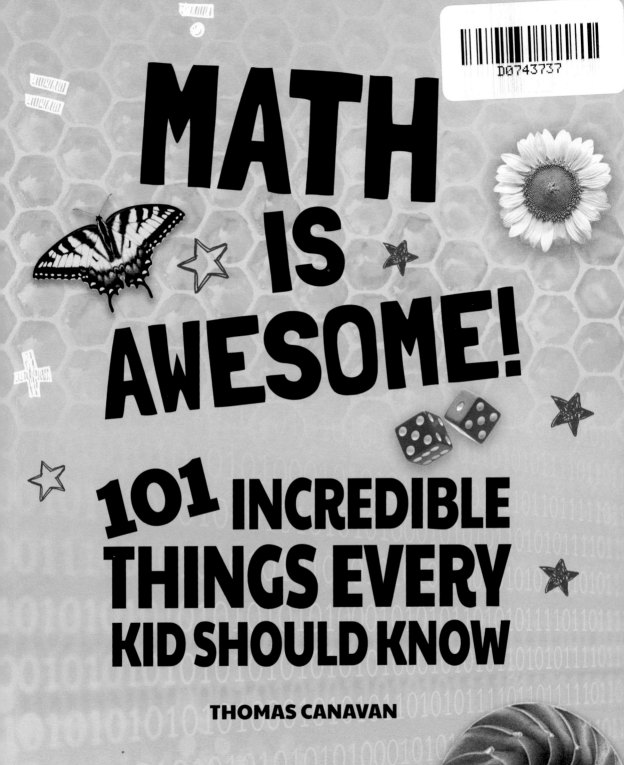

MATH IS AWESOME!

101 INCREDIBLE THINGS EVERY KID SHOULD KNOW

THOMAS CANAVAN

ARCTURUS

ARCTURUS

This edition published in 2018 by Arcturus Publishing Limited
26/27 Bickels Yard, 151–153 Bermondsey Street,
London SE1 3HA

Picture credits: 41b Dvortygirl; 93 U.S. Navy photo by Photographer's
Mate 1st Class Shane T. McCoy; 114 U.S. Navy photo by Aviation Warfare
Systems Operator 2nd Class William S. Stevens. All other images from
Shutterstock and NASA. 15b InnaFelker; 27t Aspen Photo; 36 S-F; 41
t AJP; 43t pcruciatti; 43b ermess 51t purplequeue; 83b meunierd; 87b
A.RICARDO; 97b s_bukley; 101t Rašo; 106 Dmitry Morgan; 107b Gina
Smith; 110 Carine06; 111b Jason and Bonnie Grower; 113b Maxim
Petrichuk; 119t Eddau; 122 Ververidis Vasilis;123t Darren Brode/
Shutterstock.com

Every effort has been made to trace and contact copyright holders. If
there are any inadvertent omissions we apologise to those concerned,
and would be grateful to be notified of any corrections that should be
incorporated in future reprints or editions of this book.

ISBN: 978-1-78599-873-7
CH004678US
Supplier 26, Date 0318, Print run 6909

Printed in China

Introduction

Math is AMAZING!

From counting the days of the week to measuring out ingredients for a cake—math is everywhere! Without realizing it, you use math for all sorts of different reasons throughout the day, every day. This book contains more than 100 amazing facts about math in all kinds of places and subjects—from time travel to 3-D printers, dance to outer space, the pyramids of Egypt to the Mona Lisa.

Why do we count in numbers from 0 to 9? What has the Fibonacci sequence got to do with sunflowers? Can we use our bodies to measure things? All of these questions and many more will open your eyes to the incredibly exciting world of math. Read on... and happy counting!

MATH IS A LANGUAGE WE ALL UNDERSTAND

Math can help us work out how many days there are until the holidays or how tall we are. But most of all, it helps us make sense of the world—and the vast universe. And it's the same language everywhere.

Building blocks of math

People sometimes describe mathematics as a language. It's not really a language that people speak in the street, like English or Japanese, but it does have many things in common with spoken languages. You can think of complicated calculations as books, and simpler ones as words. And what about the "letters" that lie at the heart of this language? Simple—those are the numbers.

$\div$ 1 4 8 62 994 + = $\times$ 71 88 4

781422 =

55 32 +

Things that count

Try getting by without using number words to describe things around you. Instead of saying "four trees," you might say "tree tree tree tree." That works pretty well if you're counting small amounts, but it's no good as a way of describing anything larger. Imagine, for example, trying to describe the number of bees in a swarm or grains of sand sifting through your fingers. Number systems help us solve that problem.

THERE ARE ABOUT 6,500 DIFFERENT LANGUAGES SPOKEN AROUND THE WORLD, BUT NEARLY EVERYONE CAN READ THIS: 0, 1, 2, 3, 4, 5, 6, 7, 8, 9.

Around the world

We can rely on math even when our surroundings are unfamiliar. Imagine visiting a new country—the language may be different, but you will see that the money has its value in numbers as well as words, the prices in stores are a clear amount, and you can recognize your hotel room number. Math will help you get to know your new surroundings.

FACT
2

We know of only one language with no "number words." Its speakers live deep in the Amazon jungle.

Tiny differences

Really big numbers help us work with huge amounts, such as the number of stars in the sky or a computer's memory. But numbers can also shed light on tiny amounts. These might be describing small lengths, like the size of germs. Numbers can also divide time into tiny fragments—which is useful when judging how fast a sprinter has run.

STONE AGE PEOPLE WERE GREAT AT MATH

Counting must have been one of the first skills our ancestors learned. Counting the number of animals in a herd, or the number of moons until the end of the summer, was vital to human survival.

Let's see. If both fish are swimming at 10 feet per second...

The hunt for math

Counting is the foundation of many math skills. If our ancestors could count then they could probably multiply, use fractions, understand geometrical shapes, and make accurate estimates. Getting these things right was hugely important.

FACT
4

The Sumerian people developed the first number symbols around the same time they wrote their first alphabet: about 5,500 years ago.

Seeds of knowledge

As people moved from hunting to farming, they needed more complicated math. They started to work with larger numbers than just "two deer" or "six salmon." Farmers had to decide how much of their crop could be eaten and how much should be saved to plant next year. Bartering developed, which encouraged people to develop a sense of the value of an object.

How many handfuls of seed does it take to plant a field?

Tally ho!

Before most people could read or write, pieces of bone or wood helped them keep a tally, or count, of things. The earliest tally sticks date back more than 30,000 years and have been found in Africa, Europe, and Asia. More recent sticks—from about 1,000 years ago—helped buyers and sellers work out prices. Some people (like prisoners!) still use tally marks to keep track of things.

Ancient times tables

Bamboo strips uncovered in 2014 showed that Chinese people were doing multiplication more than 2,200 years ago. As well as showing how to multiply numbers up to 100, the bamboo had instructions on how to work with fractions. These marks helped villagers to divide portions of grain for use in the winter months.

WE SET OUR CLOCKS TO BABYLONIAN TIME

"**F**ifty-seven, fifty-eight, fifty-nine... zero."
Has your clock's second hand gone crazy?
What happened to sixty, sixty-one, and all the
rest of the numbers? The answer is base-ic—
and it takes us back in time.

Back to Babylon

Our numbering system is based
on the number 10— the system
is even called "base ten." For us,
things build up in tens: ten ones
become ten, ten tens become a
hundred, ten hundreds become...
you know the rest. But the
Babylonian people in the Middle
East, living about 5,000 years
ago, used a different base—60.
This system lives on in a few
places, like how we tell time.

THE BABYLONIANS
TOOK THEIR NUMBERING
SYSTEM FROM AN
EARLIER PEOPLE —
THE SUMERIANS.

Making it count

The Babylonians started with a single mark for "1," then two marks for "2" and all the way up to nine marks for "9." Ten got its own mark, then 11 became "10 + 1 mark," 12 became "10 + 2 marks."... until number 59—five "10 marks" + "9 marks." It started again at 60, which was the same mark as "1" but in the next column.

FACT 6

"Minutes" and "seconds" are used to measure where things are on Earth.

Babylonians marked numbers in clay tablets about the size of playing cards.

Around and around

Base 60 is still used in many measurements "around" things—either around a clock (60 seconds and 60 minutes) or in the way our planet is measured. Like a circle, the world is divided into 360 degrees, and then each of those degrees (¹⁄₃₆₀th of the way around the world) is divided into 60 minutes and then 60 seconds.

Time and place

This means that the same word, second, can be used to measure angles and lengths of a circle as well as time. That type of second is about 100 feet (30m) when you're measuring around the widest part of the Earth.

FRACTIONS CAN BE BEAUTIFUL

You might think of tests or homework when you hear the word "fractions," but they are a simple way of expressing some of the wonders of the world around you.

They told me that this hat would look divine.

Pharaoh's fractions

The sculpted head of Nefertiti, royal wife of Egyptian Pharaoh Akhenaton, was made more than 3,000 years ago. The ancient Egyptians believed that their rulers would have a godlike beauty. And that beauty could best be represented with geometry, the branch of math devoted to shapes and angles. In particular, they tried to produce harmony, a balance between different parts of a design. This comparison can be written as a fraction.

Taking shape

To compare the distance from Nefertiti's nose to chin (call it "a") with the larger distance of chin to hat-brim ("b"), you could write "a/b," which is also a fraction. Then to compare "b" with the overall height of the head plus hat ("c"), you'd write "b/c." If you plugged in the real measurements, you'd find that $a/b = b/c$. Awesome!

YOU CAN THINK OF THE LINE BETWEEN THE TOP AND BOTTOM NUMBERS IN A FRACTION AS ANOTHER WAY OF SAYING "DIVIDED BY."

The Great Sphinx has been showing math in action for 4,500 years.

Large-scale design

The Egyptian fascination with fractions, angles, and proportions went far beyond the small-scale design of statues and headdresses. The Egyptians were builders on a huge scale, producing temples, tombs, and monuments to honor their pharaohs and gods. Designs of one construction would often be "echoed" in another nearby, with elements linked with similar angles. The overall effect demonstrated harmony and a mathematical perfection—like that of the heavens.

Egyptian fractions

All Ancient Egyptian fractions were "unitary" and were expressed as one divided by something else. So an Egyptian fraction could be ½, ⅓, or ¹⁄₁₀ but not ⅖ or ⁷⁄₁₀. To add up, you simply combined fractions of different amounts. So to make ¾ you could show ½ + ¼.

Division made easy

Egyptian fractions might seem clumsy in some ways, but they can be helpful when you try to divide things in real life. Imagine you want to split 7 pizzas between 10 people. Do you divide each pizza into 10 parts and give each person 7 slices? If we look at Egyptian fractions, they show that ⁷⁄₁₀ is the same as ½ + ⅕. Now we know to cut 5 pizzas in half and to cut the remaining 2 pizzas into five slices each.

11

THE ROMANS USED LETTERS FOR NUMBERS

Did Roman emperors count on their fingers? The Roman numbering system might well have started off like that, with people copying the shapes they saw as they wrote.

Pointing the finger

No matter how complicated numbers can get, we need to be able to represent them clearly. So it's easy to imagine how the Romans would have used something that everyone has: fingers. Just like children counting small numbers on their fingers, the Romans marked "I" (their number "1") down like one finger, "II" like two fingers and "III" like three fingers. Their sign for five—"V"—is the shape a hand makes when you hold up five fingers.

Roman numerals

Lovely letters

The Romans used other letters such as "C" and "M" to represent higher numbers. By combining the letters in different ways they could express almost any number. But using Roman numerals meant that adding up was a difficult and time-consuming process. Like many other people, the Romans used the abacus to help them calculate.

No need to write?

Some people have found ways to work out calculations without writing anything down. One of the oldest tools is the abacus. This is a counting frame with rows of beads that slide up and down, or across. The rows represent ones, tens, hundreds, and so on. Expert abacus users can sometimes do calculations faster than a calculator.

Listen to the numbers

Computers might soon make writing numbers down far less important. We can already speak to a computer and let it write, without having to type. A computer can listen to a math problem, solve it, and tell you the answer without your ever having to write down a single number.

ARABIC NUMBERS ARE USED EVERYWHERE

When it comes to doing complicated calculations, Roman numerals are slow and clumsy. People soon saw the advantages of working with Arabic numerals.

Making life easier

A numeral is simply a quick way of expressing a number. Today, we use the symbols "0" to "9" to express numbers, and these are called Arabic numbers. This system was developed in India, in about 500CE.

Trading up

Traders—people who buy and sell things—need to do complicated calculations quickly. Arabic traders soon saw the advantage of the Indian system. They helped to spread these numerals around the world.

Naming numbers

Numbers don't have to be expressed in numerals. We could use the words "ten thousand, two hundred, and sixty-seven" but this is time-consuming to write and not easy to work with. When a number is written down in numerals, it can be understood whatever language you speak.

SPEAKERS OF HEBREW AND ARABIC READ LETTERS FROM RIGHT TO LEFT, BUT NUMBERS FROM LEFT TO RIGHT.

FACT
11

In some languages, the words for numbers still refer to fingers and hands.

Counting in the Sotho language is as easy as looking at your hands.

Numerals everywhere

All over the world, people do advanced calculations with Arabic numerals. But when they are speaking, the language they use often has its origin in ancient terms for numbers.

Modern hand-prints

In the Sotho language of southern Africa, the word for "5" is "complete the hand," and 6 is "jump," meaning "jump to the other hand." The Klamath people, Native Americans from the Pacific coast, use similar terms that remind them of pressing their hands on the ground.

BASE 10 IS THE "HANDIEST" WAY OF COUNTING

Why did the number 10—and not 4, 7, or 12—wind up being so important for math? You can count the answer on your fingertips.

Making things count

Think of how you might count down the days until your birthday, or try to remember how many friends came to your last party. You'll probably count on your fingers (and thumbs). You run out when you reach ten, and you might even start counting again—but remembering that you've reached ten once already. There you have it: you're probably calculating like just about every human society in history, using base 10.

IF WE WERE ALL CARTOON CHARACTERS—WITH THREE FINGERS AND A THUMB ON EACH HAND—THEN WE'D PROBABLY USE BASE 8.

"Digital" thinking

Base 10 is called the decimal system. This name comes from the Latin word for "10." Everything depends on multiples of ten: ten tens become a hundred, ten hundreds become a thousand. You add a zero every time you multiply by ten. And those ten numbers that make up the base? Well, each one is called a digit, which is what doctors call a finger or a toe.

Best foot forward

If we can count with our fingers, then why not measure with other parts of the body? For centuries, people did just that. Standard measurements have replaced most of these other body part measurements, but a few linger on. People in English-speaking countries still measure horses in "hands."

A horse's height is measured in hands, from the ground to its front shoulders.

FACT 13

A British pound used to contain 240 pence instead of 100.

Easy money

Most countries use the decimal system for their money. The dollar, Euro, pound, and many other units are made up of 100 smaller bits. This system makes it easy for everyone to work out prices and amounts—even if there are lots of zeroes involved.

SOMETIMES "111" MEANS "7"

Well, it does in the binary system, which uses just two symbols, instead of our normal ten symbols, to show a quantity. It's tricky for humans but great for computers.

Marching two by two

We normally use ten symbols (0, 1, 2, 3, 4, 5, 6, 7, 8, 9) to write numbers. When we've used up all of those symbols—say, starting at 0 and going up to 9—we call the next number "10." The "1" goes up with each new set of ten, until it becomes "100." It's called Base 10. The binary system uses just two symbols (0, 1) before starting over each time. You end up with numbers with only 0s and 1s in them.

Back to basics

Computers store and send information in tiny bursts of energy. Like a light switch, this energy can be turned on or switched off. That's where the binary system suits computers. Their language is written in a series of 0s and 1s, guiding a computer to turn on or off these signals at super-high speed.

Decimal number	Binary number
1	1
2	10
3	11
4	100
5	101
6	110
7	111
8	1000
9	1001
10	1010

Bits and bytes

A computer "bit" is the smallest unit of data computers use—either a 0 or a 1. Things move up from there. A byte is 8 bits, a kilobyte is 1,000 bytes ... and the numbers keep growing.

THE WORD "BINARY" COMES FROM THE LATIN WORD "BINARIUS," MEANING "TWO TOGETHER."

Bigger and faster

Think about how hard it was to do simple arithmetic when you started school. As you learned more, you found it easier to work quickly, and with bigger numbers. Computers have "grown up" in the same way. The first home computers had memories measured in kilobytes. Now computers have memories of gigabytes (each gigabyte is 1,073,741,824 bytes), allowing them to do just about anything you can think of!

FACT 15

BABIES DO MATH ALL THE TIME

We can't all expect to become mathematical geniuses, but most of us have a basic math toolkit in our own heads. It's something we are born with—we just have to learn how to use it.

SOME PEOPLE CAN DO MATH QUICKLY IN THEIR HEAD, BUT CAN'T EXPLAIN HOW.

Setting things up

Toddlers are naturally curious and explore how things fit together—and come apart! They love to investigate the objects they see around them, moving things around and even rearranging them. Young children are able to see patterns in the world around them—and those are the building blocks of the math skills they will use later.

Does this look like an acute angle to you?

Learn while you play

It's a lot easier to learn any subject, including math, if you have some direct experience with it. And even if you don't notice it, your mind is doing math calculations even when you're playing. Think of sitting on a seesaw. If you have people balanced on either end, it's like having the same amounts on either side of the "=" in an equation.

Riding a seesaw calls for instinctive math skills.

PEOPLE SOMETIMES KNOW EXACTLY HOW MANY STAIRS THEY'VE JUST CLIMBED BECAUSE THEY WERE COUNTING IN THEIR HEADS—WITHOUT EVEN REALIZING IT.

Making predictions

A lot of math involves being able to predict what will happen if you change things around a bit. You ask yourself questions such as: "What will happen if I divide both sides of the equation by three?" "If this bit increases, something else must get smaller — right?" Of course, with time you can work the answers out "officially." But if you're lucky, you'll remember times when you've had to do those very things in real life—which may help you work out the math answers.

Share and share alike

Do you want to see a math star teach you about division, or fractions? Just watch as someone divides up a pizza for six people, or tries to give everyone the same amount of ice cream! Suddenly the room is full of math experts—and they're using their math skills in a practical, and tasty, way.

ONE THIRD OF ALL NUMBERS START WITH "1"

Numbers sometimes behave in strange ways. But there is always a logical explanation for the patterns we see.

Low numbers are winners

If you had time to look at lots of groups of numbers, you would find something very odd. Almost one third of numbers would begin with the digit 1. About another third of numbers would begin with the digits 2 or 3. Only 5% of numbers would begin with the digit 9. This odd fact is known as Benford's Law.

The number one wins again!

Lots of lists

Benford's Law can be found in all sorts of data. It is true when looking at the height of skyscrapers, the length of rivers, electricity bills, addresses, and the population of cities. However, it does not work if the data is limited in some way. For example, a school might only take pupils up to the age of 11. Benford's Law would not apply to the age of children in that school.

FACT 17

You can use math skills to help you pick a car and not a goat.

The Monty Hall Problem

Monty Hall was the host of the TV game show *Let's Make a Deal.* Mathematicians came up with a puzzle based on the program and called it the Monty Hall Problem. Imagine three doors. Behind two of the doors are goats and behind the other is a car (that's the prize you want to win.) You pick one of the doors. Your host then opens one of the other doors to reveal a goat and then asks you if you want to swap doors. Do you stick with your original choice or do you swap to the other door?

The answer is obvious

It seems as though both doors have an equal chance of containing the car. In fact, by swapping to the other door you improve your chances of winning. When you chose your original door you had a ⅓ chance of winning. If you choose to switch doors, you then have a ⅔ chance of winning. This is because the door the host opens is not random; it is <u>never</u> the door the contestant chose and it <u>always</u> contains a goat.

SOME PEOPLE ADD UP JUST BY WAVING

Most people can work out simple math problems in their head. But some people have special methods to take mental arithmatic to a whole new level.

A MENTAL MATH CHAMPION CAN ADD UP 15 THREE-DIGIT NUMBERS IN LESS THAN TEN SECONDS.

All in the mind

Some people can multiply and divide 10-digit numbers within seconds. Waving hands or fingers in front of their eyes helps them imagine the columns of an abacus, a calculating device. Their "mental abacus" works out the answer.

Why so fast?

The "mental abacus" technique lets people go straight to an image of the number (such as "327"). This is a lot more efficient than thinking of the number in words ("three hundred and twenty-seven"). People who use the mental abacus technique can calculate accurately, even if they are doing something else at the same time.

Repeat performances

Engineers often do hundreds of calculations with just the tiniest differences between them. They help determine how equipment will behave when it's used over and over. The tests might change the size of the equipment slightly, or the angles that join them. Being able to do quick math in your head is a very useful tool for engineers and people in similar jobs.

Part of an engineer's job is making quick and accurate calculations.

Other tools

Learning quick ways of doing mental calculation is a great skill. Teachers often encourage their students to go back to the first things they learned in math, such as working with number lines or breaking numbers down (so that 79 becomes 70 + 9).

FACT 19

It's easier to remember long numbers if you divide them into three- or four-digit chunks.

FACT 20
WE DO MATH INSTINCTIVELY

"**W**ell, why did I have all of those math classes?" you might say. Not everything about math is instinctive, but many elements are. It's also a matter of repetition and practice... all helping to make you a math whizz!

Math without words

Many of our math skills are innate (with us from birth) or unconscious. In other words, we're working things out or calculating almost without noticing it. Scientists tested babies by playing them a certain number of cooing sounds. Then they observed as the babies were shown a series of different shapes on a screen. Most babies stopped and concentrated on the number of shapes that matched the number of cooing sounds.

I'm a math genius already!

In-flight calculator

Just as planes have computers to help guide them, our bodies rely on our brains to control things. Many activities happen without our thinking about them at all—our hearts beat, our lungs breathe, and we make constant calculations of speed and balance as we go about our day.

Putting it all together

A tennis player hears the opponent's racket hit the ball and calculates how long it will take to reach her. A cyclist judges the angle of a hill to see how fast the bike will roll downhill, and when to put on the brakes. They're not consciously "thinking" about these actions, but practice has helped their brains do the calculations.

Muscle memory

People are aware of "muscle memory," the way in which certain skills (playing musical scales, juggling balls) become easier the more our muscles have practice doing them. After a while, we no longer need to think about them. It's likely that our brains work in the same way, calculating things all the time because they've done similar calculations a lot already.

BAD MATH SINKS SHIPS

Getting your math wrong at school can be annoying, but in the real world, errors can be far more serious. And sometimes, there's no hiding the fact that you've made a mistake.

IN 2013, A SIMPLE MATH ERROR MEANT A BRAND-NEW SUBMARINE WEIGHED TEN TIMES MORE THAN EXPECTED.

The wrong ruler

In 1628, the Swedish flagship, Vasa, was launched. Just a mile into her first voyage, the ship sank. What went wrong? The hull was thicker on one side than the other, causing the ship to be unbalanced. The workmen were using different rulers: the Swedish rulers were 12 inches long but the Amsterdam rulers were only 11 inches long.

Keeping things real

Imagine working out how tall someone is. You can probably predict that the answer will be pretty close to your own height. But if you wind up with a number that seems ten times greater than your height, or twenty times smaller, it's time to examine the order in which you worked things out.

If something looks wrong it probably is wrong!

> OPERATIONS ARE THE THINGS WE DO TO NUMBERS. THE MOST BASIC FOUR ARE ADDITION, SUBTRACTION, MULTIPLICATION, AND DIVISION.

Where to begin?

Even the best mathematicians usually stop and look at a problem before plunging in. It could be something as simple as:

$$7 \times 5 - 2$$

Do you work from left to right? Right to left? Does it matter? Should you do 7×5 first, so the answer is 33? Or should the $5 - 2$ come first, making the answer 21? Luckily, people have accepted rules about how to work these problems out.

FACT 22

You can add and multiply in any order.
$7 + 2$ is the same as $2 + 7$
7×2 is the same as 2×7

Time to operate?

The general agreement in working out calculations is called the "order of operations." It helps you decide where to begin, and where to go from there. The simplest rule says multiply or divide before you add or subtract. So in this example, you should do the 7×5 first, and then subtract the 2. Even the more complicated operations "know their place" in calculations.

Now, where to start with this problem...?

29

ALL THE BEST MATHEMATICIANS CHEAT

Some questions seem almost impossible to answer. But are you sure you are looking at the problem in the right way? Sometimes tackling a problem using a different method will give you the answer you want.

How high is a pyramid?

Thales was an mathematician in ancient Greece. He wanted to find out the height of a pyramid but he couldn't climb to the top. The problem seemed to be impossible, but Thales "cheated." He measured the height of the pyramid's shadow. And he chose to do it at the time of day when his own shadow was equal to his height. Sneaky!

APPROACHING A TOUGH PROBLEM FROM A DIFFERENT ANGLE IS CALLED LATERAL THINKING.

Approaching a problem

Deciding on the best way of approaching a problem is half the battle in solving it. Teachers are right to say "read each question carefully." It's often a matter of choosing the best "route" to the solution. Then it's time to decide which math operation will reveal the answer: addition, subtraction, multiplication, or division. The answer is the destination. But where to start?

Which way to go? There is often no "right" way—just different routes.

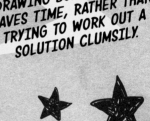

GOING "BACK TO THE DRAWING BOARD" OFTEN SAVES TIME, RATHER THAN TRYING TO WORK OUT A SOLUTION CLUMSILY.

FACT 24

Sometimes the best way to subtract is to start by adding a number.

Helpful U-turns

Because we work in base 10, it's easy to add or subtract ten from a number. Some of the best shortcuts lead you there. Here's one: if you're subtracting 5 from a number, start by adding 5. That's usually pretty easy. Then subtract 10!

Away from the classroom

Don't think you'll ever need to do quick math calculations? Think again. Your luggage is 5 lb too heavy at the airport. How many hardback books (each weighing 15 oz) need to come out? Shoes (1 lb a pair)? Paperbacks (10 oz each)? Can you get a combination of these out and fit them into your hand luggage? Hurry—your flight's being called!

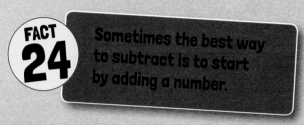

THE EARTH IS ROUND— AND WE CAN PROVE IT!

The tool we use is geometry, the branch of math that deals with shapes and angles. Think of a ship disappearing over the horizon and you'll understand.

Out of sight

For centuries people have noticed that ships don't just seem to get smaller before disappearing. They actually seem to "sink" over the horizon, until only the tallest part of the mast can be seen. That fact can get you thinking about curves and angles... which is where geometry takes over. If you had a way of telling how far the ship had sailed—and how tall the mast was—you could learn a lot about Earth.

THE PART OF THE SEA CLOSEST TO THE HORIZON IS CALLED THE "OFFING."

Shadowy calculations

Eratosthenes, a Greek astronomer, calculated the Earth's circumference more than 2,000 years ago. He compared the angles of shadows cast in two Egyptian cities at noon on the longest day of the year. The tiny difference showed how much of the circle (the Earth) — about $1/50$th — lay between the two cities. He knew the surface distance between them and multiplied by 50 to get the answer.

Not far off

Eratosthenes' calculations gave him the answer 28,968 miles (46,620 km). Modern measurements using highly accurate machines put the Earth's circumference at 24,901 miles (40,075 km). So Eratosthenes was impressively close for a first go!

FACT
26

An understanding of geometry saves forests from fire.

Fire!

Putting it into practice

You can use some circumference calculations "backward." For example, many parts of the world rely on watchtowers to prevent forest fires. These watchtowers are built high, so firefighters can watch over a large area. But how large? If you know that you can work out how high you need to build that tower.

YOU CAN USE PI TO MEASURE A PIE

And not just a pie. You can use pi to measure the distance around any circle. All you need is two numbers—the width across the circle and the number pi.

A MATHEMATICAL CONSTANT IS ALWAYS THE SAME, BUT IS USED TO HELP MANY DIFFERENT CALCULATIONS.

Constant help

The length around a circle is called its circumference and its width is called its diameter. More than 3,500 years ago, people in Egypt and China noted that dividing the circumference by the diameter always came up with the same number, just over 3. We now call this special number pi, which is how we spell the Greek letter π. Pi is the most famous example of a constant, or unchanging, number.

Just resting in this circumference...

Calculating pi

The best way to find out the value of pi is to take a really accurate measure of a circumference and divide it by the diameter. It would be great if the answer came out as a whole number, or even one where the decimal places stop. But it just keeps on going... and going. That puts pi in a special math category—it's known as an irrational number. This means that it can't be expressed neatly as a fraction. Some people round pi to the fraction $^{22}/_7$, but that's just an estimate... and starts to go wrong after about the third decimal place.

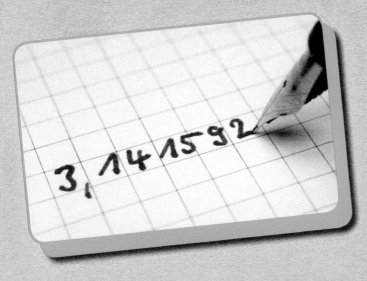

MATHEMATICIANS CALCULATED PI TO 10 TRILLION DECIMAL PLACES IN 2011.

Out of this world

You can use pi to work out the circumference of a sphere, which is really a circle in three dimensions: length, width, and height. The widest part of a sphere (like the Equator running around the Earth) is really a circle. That's how scientists can calculate the circumference of distant planets once they've measured how far they are across.

Shaping up

Pi is used to help calculate lots of things beyond just circumferences. For one thing, it can help work out areas (the space inside two-dimensional objects like circles) and volumes (the space inside three-dimensional objects like spheres). You can use pi to measure any object that has a circular base—even the volume of ice cream that is, or was, in your cone.

THE MONA LISA IS FULL OF MATH SECRETS

Leonardo da Vinci, the artist who painted the famous Mona Lisa, was fascinated by math. You can draw imaginary lines across his paintings to see mathematical shapes such as circles, triangles, and rectangles.

Clever blend

Leonardo da Vinci lived in the 15th century, at a time when Europeans were developing ideas about how to represent things in art. The result was an exciting mixture of beauty and balance, and many people came to believe that the most beautiful things displayed balance and proportion—both of which rely on math. It's not surprising that this interest in math led Leonardo into architecture and invention as well.

Mysteries behind the smile

The Golden Ratio is a mathematical constant (like pi) that Leonardo knew about. Imagine dividing a line unevenly so that the longer section divided by the shorter comes up with the same number as the whole line divided by the longer section. This number (about 1.62) figures in many of da Vinci's paintings. It's also the length of Mona Lisa's face divided by the width.

A matter of perspective

When we look at a photograph of a road stretching straight off into the distance, the road appears to become narrower. But we know that it remains the same width in real life. This is called perspective. Leonardo and fellow Renaissance painters introduced perspective in their paintings.

Natural balance

Two centuries before the Mona Lisa, another Italian named Leonardo Fibonacci noticed something odd about the number sequence 0, 1, 1, 2, 3, 5, 8, 13 and so on. Each number is the sum of the previous two. We call this sequence Fibonacci numbers. And each number divided by the previous one leads to... the golden ratio!

WE CAN DRAW THE FIBONACCI NUMBERS AS A SERIES OF RECTANGLES. TAKE A SQUARE (1), ADD ANOTHER SQUARE (1) AND YOU MAKE A RECTANGLE (2). ADD ANOTHER SQUARE (3) AND THEN ANOTHER (5) AND THEN ADD ONE MORE (8)... AND SO ON!

Painting by numbers?

The sequence of Fibonacci numbers can form a series of shapes that grow into bigger and bigger squares, rectangles, and circles. Some scientists believe that our brains "expect" the next Fibonacci shape just as we expect "ti" and "do" at the end of a musical scale. Artists often group objects to sit within this series.

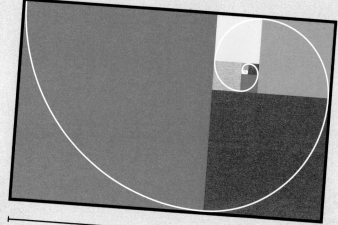

$$(a+b)/a = a/b = 1.61803...$$

37

We call something symmetrical if it can be flipped, sliced through, or rotated, and still look the same. Understanding symmetry helps engineers with their designs, and some of the best inspiration comes from nature.

Going for a spin

The starfish is an ideal example of rotational symmetry. Imagine finding one on the beach. You could carefully pick it up and move it a one-fifth turn (that's where the rotation is coming in) and put it down again. It would still look the same. And you could do that five times and get the same result. But you'd fail if you tried to do the same thing with an oyster shell or a lobster.

MOST PEOPLE'S FACES ARE NOT QUITE SYMMETRICAL, DESPITE WHAT WE MIGHT THINK.

Formal gardens owe as much to math as to biology.

Natural symmetry

The starfish is an example of symmetry in nature. We come across many other examples of symmetry every day, from the patterns of a cat's coat to our own bodies (both halves would look similar if we were sliced down the middle). Sometimes people "repay this compliment," planting gardens to display perfect symmetry.

Mirror images

Although symmetry can become very complicated and advanced, it's also one of the first math concepts that children understand. The most basic symmetry, called reflective symmetry, is about one line of symmetry. Think of it next time you look in the mirror.

FACT 30

Soccer players calculate the movement of a truncated icosahedron.

Check out my icosahedron kicking skills!

On the ball math

A soccer ball looks like a sphere, but really it is a shape of 32 sides, made up from pentagons and hexagons which slot together neatly. Imagine a solid shape with 20 triangular faces (this is called an icosahedron). If you cut off (truncate) the 12 corners of the icosahedron you wind up with 12 pentagons and 20 hexagons. In other words, a soccer ball!

PEOPLE CAN USE THEIR BODIES AS RULERS

Whether it's our hands, feet, or fingers, people have always looked to their bodies to measure the world around them. Even in the age of smartphones, we still look for what's familiar.

Getting the measure

A fisherman describing "the one that got away" won't say that the fish was "about five feet long." He'll throw his arms out wide to show you how big it was. Some of the oldest measurements were based on the length of a king's forearm or finger. And the words "hands" and "feet" are still used to describe units of length.

A "TALL TALE" TAPE MEASURE MAKES A CATCH LOOK LONGER THAN IT REALLY IS.

Shaving distance

Who said math couldn't be fun, or funny? Scientists love to come up with new measurements, sometimes based on things that can be observed (but usually aren't). A "beard second" is a tiny unit of length — it's the amount that a man's beard grows in one second.

Shrinking buildings

When adults go back to their childhood schools everything often seems to be smaller than they remember it. That's because they still have strong memories of the how big the buildings were compared to their own size as children.

FACT 32

A bridge in Boston is measured in "smoots."

An orange line marks the 100-smoot point of Harvard Bridge.

The strangest measurement?

The sidewalk along the Harvard Bridge in Boston, Massachusetts, is marked off in regular intervals called "smoots." The measurement arose in 1958, when a group of students measured the bridge using one of their friends, Oliver Smoot, as a ruler. The "10-smoot" marks along the bridge have been repainted many times. A sign at the end gives the distance: "364.4 smoots, plus one ear."

OLIVER SMOOT RETIRED IN 2005. HE HAD BEEN CHAIRMAN OF THE AMERICAN NATIONAL STANDARDS INSTITUTE, WHICH LOOKS AFTER... MEASUREMENTS.

FACT 33

LAND CAN BE MEASURED IN "OXEN DAYS"

Some modern measurements date back to ancient ways of life. They're a form of math history to help explain our past.

Team players

Many agricultural societies measure land in ways that were easily understood by farmers. In Britain and America an "acre" is the amount of field that a team of oxen could plow in a single day. In Poland and Germany a "morgen" is the amount of land that could be plowed in a morning by a single man and an ox. Other countries measure using the things that are important to them: in Japan, land is measured in "tsubo," which is the area covered by a traditional floor mat.

SCOTTISH, WELSH, AND IRISH MILES WERE ONCE DIFFERENT LENGTHS—AND ALL WERE LONGER THAN ENGLISH MILES.

International sports all use the metric system.

The dawn of metric

In 1791, the French government voted to establish a standard unit of length—the meter. It was to be one ten-millionth of one-quarter of the Earth's circumference. Surveyors worked from northern France to southern Spain to get a precise measurement. Eight years later they produced an "end bar" made of platinum. It became the standard for the new metric system.

Stadium events

Olympic events are measured in units based on the modern metric system. Whether it's the 200 m backstroke, the women's 10 km biathlon, or 120 kg weights being lifted, the measurements are the same everywhere. One of the most popular running events, the 1500 m, is sometimes called the "metric mile" because it tests runners in the same way as the traditional mile run.

IN ANCIENT GREECE, THE OLYMPICS CONSISTED OF A SINGLE EVENT— A SPRINT ALONG THE LENGTH OF THE STADIUM.

Old-fashioned race

Each year dozens of old-fashioned cars take part in a race across the Italian countryside. The race is called the "Miglia mille." It means "one thousand miles." Italy has used the metric system for more than 200 years, so using the cast-off measurement "miles" adds to the old-time atmosphere of the race.

A LIGHT-YEAR MEASURES LENGTH, NOT TIME

The distances between objects in the universe are so big that we call huge numbers "astronomical." But we also have ways of measuring those distances without running out of zeroes.

PROXIMA CENTAURI, THE NEAREST STAR TO OUR SUN, IS 4.24 LIGHT-YEARS AWAY.

Easier units

The best way to "get a handle" on those distances is to use the speed of light, which is 983,571,056 feet per second. Then calculate how far that same light would travel in a year (a light-year). You'd need to multiply that big number by 60 (to find a light-minute), then 60 (hour), then 24 (day) and then 365. That means a light-year is 31, 039, 143, 016, 731, 900 feet, or about 5.88 trillion miles.

FACT 35

The Sun is eight light-minutes away from Earth.

Crooked orbits

Most planets have orbits that are ellipses, like slightly flattened circles. The Earth's distance from the Sun varies from 91.5 million miles to 94.5 million miles each year. Other planets' orbits vary even more.

Vast distances

The Earth sits about 93 million miles from the Sun. That's a huge number, but that same distance is just a tiny fraction of the distance from the Sun to Neptune, the outermost planet in our solar system. And that distance is nothing compared to the distances between stars and galaxies. The zeroes would spill off the page if we kept using miles. So that's why light-years are so handy.

Some telescopes "see" things 100 million light-years away.

The right angle

The night sky is like a semicircle, which can be measured in angles (degrees, minutes, and seconds). Scientists use those angles to calculate distances between Earth and stars. They compare the position of the star at two different times, six months apart. The more distant the star, the less its apparent position will change. They then convert the angle into a unit of distance called a parsec, which is equal to 3.26 light-years.

To infinity and beyond?

If the universe has no outer edge, it just goes on and on and on. That boundless idea, or infinity, is also the "destination" of decimals that go on and on, like pi.

A JIFFY IS A REAL UNIT OF TIME

It might seem like a funny word to describe a precise measurement, but mathematicians and scientists like to smile too. And behind the smile is an intention to learn what makes things tick.

Chopping up time

For many centuries, farming and fishing communities had no real need to know much more than days, weeks, months, and years. Things have changed, and modern technology has led us to define—or even invent—exact units of time. "Jiffy" once meant a lightning flash, but American chemist Gilbert Lewis proposed that it should define the time it takes for light to travel one centimeter. He was half-serious, but the title remained.

GILBERT LEWIS ALSO CAME UP WITH THE WORD "PHOTON" TO DESCRIBE TINY PARTICLES OF LIGHT.

Gone in a flash

Scientists are always looking for more precise units of measurement. And it's the behavior of tiny particles—smaller than atoms—that give the basis of some very detailed units. The smallest unit of time is called Planck Time. It's the time it takes for a photon (a particle of light) to travel one Planck length, or 0.00000000000000000000000000000000000053 feet.

Julian Dates

Because people have used so many different calendars through history, astronomers sometimes use Julian Dates to avoid confusion. These refer to the number of days that have passed since January 1, 4713BCE. The Julian Date for January 1, 2018 will be 2458119.500000.

Some traditional jobs don't call for split-second timing.

FACT 37

A dinosaur's day was shorter than ours.

Give or take an hour

Many units of time are based on our planet's relationship with the Moon, the Sun, and other objects in the universe. Whether it's a year based on our path around the Sun, or the Moon's orbit creating months, it's all about movement. But the Earth's spin is slowing down, so a "day" was an hour shorter millions of years ago.

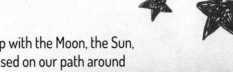

NIAGARA FALLS FILLS 7,500 TUBS A SECOND

But only if you could line up all the bath tubs. The official figure for the flow of the Niagara Falls is 750,000 gallons per second.

Go with the flow

That's a lot of tubs. Or gallons. Both measurements are useful to scientists. It's important to be able to express the amount using precise terms such as "gallons" but also to find terms that make the amount easier to picture and understand (bath tubs).

Small-scale models help us to understand large-scale objects.

Keeping it "real"

Most people wouldn't answer, "Oh, about 5 feet" if someone asked how tall their new refrigerator was. They'd probably say "a bit taller than my dad (or brother)" to give a clearer picture of the height. We like to use familiar images as measurements in conversation, which is why amounts are often compared to football pitches, double-decker buses, or even Olympic swimming pools.

Heavens above

Measurements that seem too big to understand are sometimes described as being "astronomical"—referring to the vast distances in space. It can be helpful to use models that depict distances and objects on a manageable scale. Some 18th-century models of the solar system were like works of art.

THE FIRST KNOWN MECHANICAL MODEL OF THE HEAVENS WAS BUILT IN GREECE ABOUT 2,300 YEARS AGO.

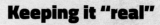

I hope no one's going to be taller than 2 inches!

"Scaling up"

Architects also find it easier to work when they have a clear picture of the building they are working on. They do this by creating scale models that are in the same proportion to the finished work. You don't want to build a skyscraper in an office. But a model 2 feet tall would be a useful way of demonstrating its design and features.

OUR CALENDARS HAVE "LOST" 11 DAYS SINCE 1582

That's when the modern calendar began to spread through the world. Today's calendar is much more accurate, but 11 days had to be trimmed to make it work.

Drifting away

In the late 1500s, scientists and religious leaders agreed that the calendar was "out" by about 11 minutes a year. Over many years, this error had turned into days. Pope Gregory XIII called on countries to adopt the accurate ("Gregorian") calendar to help Church holidays return to their original season. For example, Easter had drifted well away from its origins at the start of spring.

RUSSIA HELD OUT UNTIL THE 1920S: ITS FAMOUS "OCTOBER REVOLUTION" IS NOW MARKED IN NOVEMBER.

Ahh! Where did all that time go?!

Diary

It's called Oktoberfest but it happens in September.

Where's the time gone?

Strange things occurred as some countries adopted the new calendar and others stuck with the older Julian calendar. You could sail from France and arrive 11 days earlier in England. And when Britain did adopt the Gregorian calendar in 1752, some people rioted because they'd lost all those days. Germany's famous Oktoberfest takes place in September because it began before the calendar change.

Written in the stars

Calendars aren't just random whims invented by humans. They need to match the movement of the Earth in relation to the Sun and the Moon in relation to the Earth. Modern instruments can ensure that we begin each new year, and season, precisely when we should.

 **FACT 40**

You could finish college before your sixth birthday.

Leap years

Even the Gregorian calendar needs adjustments to match the Earth's movement. Every four years (with some rare exceptions) we add an extra day at the end of February to make a leap year. A person born on February 29 could be 24 years old but would have only celebrated six birthdays. And imagine what happens to twins born either side of midnight on February 28-29!

MATH MIGHT HELP US TALK TO SPACE ALIENS

"Is anybody out there?," we ask as we look at the thousands of stars in the night sky. But if anybody—or anything—is there, they probably won't speak an Earth language. Maybe math will provide a link.

Picking up signals

Super-sensitive radio telescopes help scientists gather information from outer space. They use math to try to find patterns in the signals. Most of those patterns were probably produced naturally. Perhaps one day they will pick up a real communication—and someone might pick up one of our signals, like your favorite television show.

ASTRONOMERS HAVE FOUND PLANETS THAT ARE CLOSE IN SIZE TO EARTH AND A SIMILAR DISTANCE FROM THEIR SUN.

Math chat

So if an alien doesn't speak English, how would we communicate? We could use binary language (a series of 1s and 0s) or prime numbers to create patterns. But so far, these are just ideas. There are no signs of intelligent life beyond our planet, although scientists continue to look...

We can work it out

Powerful telescopes can calculate the movements of distant objects. Some stars have a tiny "wiggle," which comes from the pull of an orbiting planet. Although the planets are too small for us to see, astronomers can work out their size and distance from the star.

Out of this world

If we want to go looking for life elsewhere, we need to explore our neighbors first. Setting up bases on even the closest planet, Mars, calls for complicated calculations . There's no room for error when you're that far away.

Zero gravity can be fun!

FACT 42

In 1961, a mathematician invented a formula to predict the number of intelligent alien civilizations. He thought there might be 18 million!

FACT 43
A DAY LASTS LONGER THAN A DAY

Wait—that doesn't make sense! But in fact it does, as long as you know that there are different types of day, even on our own planet. Math can show the difference.

The solar day

Our 24-hour day is the time between the Sun's highest point on one day (noon) until its highest point on the next day. While the Earth spins on its axis, it is also orbiting the Sun. In the time it takes to spin around once, the Earth travels $1/366$ of its way around the Sun. It takes another $1/366$ of a rotation (about 4 minutes) to get the Sun to appear back in the same place in the sky. Add those minutes to the "day" and you get the 24-hour solar day.

AIRCRAFT NEED TO CALCULATE THE EARTH'S SPIN WHEN THEY FLY NORTH–SOUTH.

Look to the stars

So a day is 24 hours—right? Well, not exactly. The Earth is tilted so that the North Pole points almost exactly toward a star called Polaris. And it still points at Polaris no matter where the Earth is in its orbit around the Sun. If you looked at Polaris long enough, you'd see the stars seeming to spin around it. And one complete spin—meaning that our Earth has rotated once—takes 23 hours, 56 minutes. This version of a day is called a sidereal day.

A night photo shows stars "spinning" around Polaris.

THE FOUR-MINUTE DIFFERENCES BETWEEN THE TYPES OF DAY ADD UP. EVERY FOUR YEARS WE ADD A WHOLE EXTRA DAY: A LEAP YEAR.

Off kilter

The Earth is tilted to the side at an angle of about 23 degrees. If the Earth spun parallel to the plane of its orbit—like an upright spinning top on a table—the poles would be perpendicular, jutting straight up and down. The amount of daylight in a day would be the same all year round.

FACT
44

A pendulum can demonstrate the Earth's rotation.

Swing low

If you could get a pendulum to swing long enough, you could see proof that the Earth spins on its axis. The pendulum would stay true its path, but the Earth would spin beneath it. A French mathematician, Leon Foucault, first demonstrated this effect in 1851.

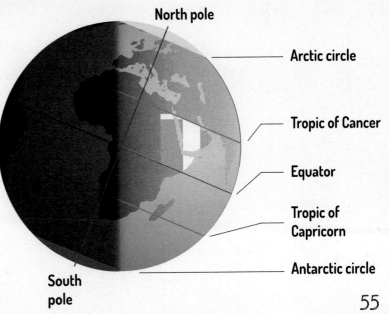

North pole

Arctic circle

Tropic of Cancer

Equator

Tropic of Capricorn

Antarctic circle

South pole

55

YOUR PHONE COULD GUIDE A MOON ROCKET

Next time you pull out your phone, think about the computing power it has. To engineers working with the most advanced computers of 50 years ago, your phone would seem like science fiction!

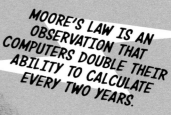

MOORE'S LAW IS AN OBSERVATION THAT COMPUTERS DOUBLE THEIR ABILITY TO CALCULATE EVERY TWO YEARS.

Warning: low memory

The first humans to land on the Moon completed their journey across 240,000 miles (386,000 km) of space, and back again, in 1969. The Apollo Guidance Computer (AGC) plotted their course and speed. It had 64 kilobytes of memory, compared with about 1 megabyte of memory in a typical smartphone. That means that your phone is 16 times more powerful than the AGC!

The sky's the limit

When you count your change in a store or work out how long it will take to cycle home, you're doing calculations. They're the nuts and bolts of mathematics, the way in which we put our learning into practice. But no matter how clever or educated we are, many jobs call for more calculation than we can manage. That's where computers have stepped in, and your smartphone's tiny computer.

Better than brains?

Our brains can process 100,000,000,000,000 instructions per second and the fastest computer in the world (called "Roadrunner") can work through ten times as many. So does that mean that computers are better? It's hard to say, because the computer works on just one problem whereas our brains are dealing with information coming from millions of nerves in our body.

Will computers of the future have hologram screens?

Moving on

As computers become more powerful, smaller, and faster, some people worry that human beings will lose their ability to do math calculations. Many schools already ban phones and calculators from exam rooms. When did you last see a cashier count out change without checking what the screen said?

SATELLITES CAN GUIDE YOU UP A MOUNTAIN

The satellites orbiting over 12,400 miles (20,000 km) above Earth can pinpoint our exact location. They can help us decide what route to take, whether we are climbing a mountain or exploring a city.

Where on Earth?

We map the world using latitude (to show how far north or south places are) and longitude (east or west). Latitude and longitude are broken up into degrees, minutes, and seconds to give exact locations. A special receiver picks up radio signals from satellites high above us. These signals let the receiver calculate exactly where we are, and how to get to where we want to be.

THE SATELLITE NAVIGATION IS CALLED THE GLOBAL POSITIONING SYSTEM, OR GPS.

Eyes in the sky

About 30 communication satellites orbit (go around) the Earth. Wherever you are, at least three of them are above you. Each satellite sends a signal to your receiver, saying exactly where it is. The receiver then works out its own location (yours!) by calculating the differences between the sets of information. This kind of math is called triangulation.

Into orbit

Communication satellites, like everything orbiting the Earth (including the Moon) are actually falling toward the Earth the whole time. But they're also moving forward, which keeps them the same distance from Earth. Any faster and they'd shoot away from Earth; slower and they'd crash back down. When satellites are launched, it is crucial to get the math right.

The right wavelength

Satellites send information on radio waves, a form of energy. The distance between the waves is called the wavelength. Light is another form of energy measured by its wavelength. Different colors have different wavelengths. These can be expressed as numbers, so you can use math to calculate the difference between any color of the rainbow.

THE WAVELENGTH OF OBJECTS MOVING AWAY FROM US GETS "REDDER" (LONGER), AND WE CAN MEASURE THEIR SPEED BY HOW RED THEY ARE.

FACT 47 A MATH BOOK SAVED COLUMBUS'S LIFE

In 1504 CE, the people of Jamaica got tired of supplying food to Christopher Columbus and his hungry crew. But Columbus used the math in his almanac to persuade them to continue.

All worked out

Columbus had been stranded on the north coast of Jamaica since June 1503. His ships were leaking, and he and his crew were marooned. He asked the local people for help, but after six months or so the local people became tired of feeding the ungrateful Europeans. Luckily for Columbus, he had a book that predicted a total eclipse of the Moon. Columbus told the locals that the Moon would disappear unless they continued to help him. And when the sky did indeed grow dark, the locals promised to provide food if Columbus would call the Moon back.

Useful book

Columbus referred to his almanac to predict the eclipse. An almanac is a book containing information about weather, stars, and eclipses, all worked out mathematically. The first known almanac was compiled more than 3,200 years ago, in Egypt.

Detailed predictions can help to save coastal areas from destructive waves.

Predicting trouble

Some natural events, such as volcanic eruptions, can't be predicted. But lunar (Moon) and solar (Sun) eclipses can be predicted down to the second, years in advance, using math. It's all about calculating the movements of the Sun, Moon, and Earth. Math also helps to predict the size and course of tsunamis, huge destructive waves triggered by undersea earthquakes.

FACT 48 Math lets spacecraft "catch a lift" from other planets on long voyages.

Helpful planets

Math can help spacecraft get a boost on the most distant voyages. After detailed math calculations, the spacecraft is sent not toward its ultimate destination but toward a planet along the way. It then gets a "gravity assist," as it's drawn in by the planet's gravity and then swung out even faster on the other side.

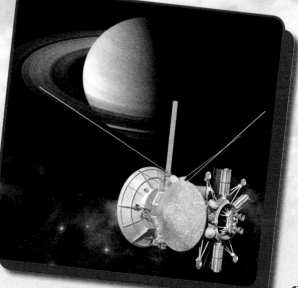

KNOWING THE RIGHT TIME SAVES LIVES

It took really accurate clocks and good math skills for sailors to navigate safely in unfamiliar waters. Before reliable clocks arrived at the end of the 18th century, ships would often sail drastically off course.

SAILORS USED (AND SOMETIMES STILL USE) INSTRUMENTS CALLED SEXTANTS TO MEASURE THE HEIGHT OF THE SUN.

Mapping the world

All maps, including modern GPS settings list latitude (north-south) and longitude (east-west) measurements. For centuries, sailors could determine latitude by measuring how high the Sun reached at noon. But the Earth's spin made it hard for them to work out how far east or west they were. And that's where the danger lay, with sharp rocks or even hostile pirates waiting for them if they got lost.

It's about time

Math helped solve the problem. For every 15 degrees that you move east, the time goes one hour ahead. And 15 degrees is ¹/₂₄th of the way around the world. So if you compare the exact time where you are with the time somewhere else in the world, you can work out how far east or west you are. In other words, your longitude.

Seasick clocks

The problem with early clocks was that they were delicate and didn't work on the high seas. But in 1764, Englishman John Harrison finally succeeded in producing a watch that lost only 40 seconds on a 47-day voyage. The "longitude problem" had been solved.

A British postage stamp honors John Harrison and his marine watch.

Prime meridian

Everyone agrees that 0 degrees is the latitude of the Equator and the two poles lie 90 degrees north and south. But with the Earth spinning, where should we put zero degrees longitude, or the prime meridian*? The answer was obvious in the 1700s. The English had the first accurate "longitude clock," so the prime meridian is in Greenwich, London.

*Each line of longitude is called a meridian, so the prime meridian is the one where you begin counting.

VISITORS TO GREENWICH, LONDON, CAN STAND ON THE PRIME MERIDIAN—WITH ONE FOOT "ON EITHER SIDE OF THE WORLD."

YOU CAN CIRCLE THE GLOBE ON A TANK OF FUEL

A car could do that, if it used a jumbo jet's fuel tank—about 50,000 gallons (190,000 liters). But let's look again at the figures: traveling by plane may not be as wasteful as you think.

A FORMULA 1 RACING CAR USES 60 GALLONS OF FUEL DURING A 186-MILE RACE. YOUR FAMILY CAR WOULD ONLY NEED ABOUT 5 GALLONS!

Scaling up and down

First off, here's a calculation. A typical car drives about 36 miles (58 km) for each gallon of fuel, so 50,000 gallons would take it 1.8 million miles (3 million km). Divide that by the Earth's circumference (about 24,800 miles/40,000 km) and you get 75 passenger trips around the world. The same amount of fuel takes the jet about 7,700 miles (12,500 km). But wait! A jumbo jet carries about 500 passengers. So between them they travel over 3.8 million miles (6 million kilometers) — the equivalent of one passenger circling the globe 156 times.

Heading for empty

You can play around with figures a bit. For example, if the car had two passengers, things would start to even out. And if it had four passengers, the car would be the winner again (300 "passenger trips "around the world). But these considerations are very important because the world will eventually run out of fuel for planes and cars, so saving it is good for the planet.

Filling your tank with gas uses fuel that will eventually run out.

A SOLAR-POWERED PLANE HAS FLOWN FROM JAPAN TO HAWAII (OVER 3,000 MILES/5,000 KM). THE NONSTOP JOURNEY TOOK ALMOST 5 DAYS.

Getting the measure

"Fuel economy," or being able to go further with the same amount of fuel, is an advantage for any vehicle. But you should use your math skills when choosing the most fuel efficient car. In some countries, people look for "miles per gallon," so a bigger number is better. Other countries work out "liters per 100 km," so economy-minded buyers look for a smaller number.

Around the world with no fuel?

Some planes, such as the "Solar Impulse," use solar panels to power their engines, so they don't use any fuel that's in short supply. Long journeys are possible, but engineers and pilots need to calculate how long the solar batteries will last and plot a course that finds a landing spot before the batteries run low—or it gets too dark to charge them.

NO ONE GETS LOST IN NEW YORK CITY

Imagine you've parachuted in to New York City, but you're not sure where you are. You simply need to look up at the street signs. The arrangement and names of New York's streets make it easy to work out your exact location.

EAU CLAIRE, WISCONSIN, HAS STREETS NUMBERED UP TO 1010 (BUT IT SKIPS A FEW NUMBERS ALONG THE WAY).

City rectangles

New York City is laid out like a grid, with "streets" running east-west and "avenues" running north-south. The street numbers work northward and the avenues are numbered from east to west. Those streets and avenues meet at right angles to form "blocks." New Yorkers judge distances by calculating the number of blocks. That math calculation lets them know whether they can walk, or whether they need to take a taxi or a bus.

No satellite needed?

GPS devices use information from communication satellites to pinpoint where they are. That's not enough to help drivers. They also need to have information about streets, roads, and natural features. Internet maps combine both to guide drivers.

Driverless cars

It's one thing to let GPS devices tell drivers where to go. The next step, of course, is to let the car drive itself. Some modern cars have built-in computers that not only receive GPS information, but also drive the car themselves without "human error." They constantly calculate distances between cars and predict how long a car will take to turn or stop.

Driverless cars can calculate speeds and distances faster than humans.

FACT 52

Satellites can lead people to "buried treasure."

Space-age treasure hunt

People taking part in the sport of geocaching can download GPS clues to help them find a hidden container (or "cache"). Once they find it, they sign their names as proof of their success. Caches can be hidden in the middle of big cities or in the remote wilderness. The computer helps calculate where things are, but players need to use their own math skills to calculate how long their hunts will take.

67

A BUTTERFLY'S WINGS CAN CAUSE HURRICANES

Then again, they might not. That uncertainty has led to the rise of a new branch of mathematics. It's known as "chaos theory" because it deals with things that are hard to predict.

UNPREDICTABILITY LIES AT THE HEART OF CHAOS THEORY. THAT'S WHY NO TWO SPORTING MATCHES ARE EXACTLY ALIKE, EVEN IF BOTH TEAMS KEEP THE SAME LINEUPS.

The "Butterfly Effect"

Until the beginning of the 20th century, people believed that all natural actions could be predicted if you had the right information. But a new theory arose, suggesting that even the smallest change in a condition (such as whether or not a butterfly flapped its wings) could lead to huge changes in outcomes (such as whether storms developed on the other side of the world). People described this as the "butterfly effect," using the flapping wings as the example.

Chaos theory

The butterfly effect was just an interesting idea... until the early 1960s. A computer expert with an interest in weather, Edward Lorenz, was setting up programs to predict weather. He noticed that if there was a tiny difference (as little as a millionth decimal place) at the start of a program, the result would change dramatically... maybe even causing "chaos"!

Chaos theory helps us predict the "random" behavior of crowds.

Test the theory

You're probably demonstrating chaos theory today. Would you have chosen that same cereal bowl if your brother had emptied the dishwasher? And would he have emptied the dishwasher if his football game had finished on time? And would the game have ended on time if the referee hadn't been stuck in traffic?

FACT 54

Chaos theory is used in medicine.

Medical math

Many things in the human body operate "like clockwork." Even before we are born, our hearts beat in a predictable rhythm. But sometimes a baby's heartbeat becomes irregular, and it's hard to know why. Doctors are now using chaos theory to work backward, and to find a reason for the abnormal heartbeat without operating. After all chaos theory tells us that events are not unpredicatable if we have enough data.

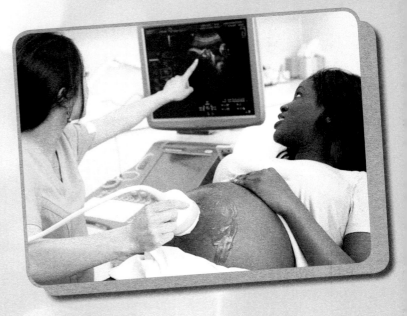

SOME SEEDS GROW IN A MATHEMATICAL PATTERN

Sunflowers might seem to have a crowded collection of seeds, but they grow in an important mathematical arrangement. And those same patterns appear in many other plants—and animals.

Natural sequence

The Fibonacci sequence (see page 37) is what you get if you start out 0, 1, and then add the last two numbers to get the next one: 1, 2, 3, 5, 8, 13, and so on. Mathematicians have divided the numbers in the sequence by the previous one. After the first three pairs (which divide neatly), you wind up with numbers that get pretty close to 1.618—but not quite exactly. That "golden ratio" (see page 36), like pi, can't be reduced to a neat fraction.

Do I detect a pattern?

A sunflower needs to cluster as many seeds as possible into its blossom. It needs to "place one, then turn" before placing the next. If its fraction of a turn (compared to a complete spin of the flower) is exact—like ¼ for example— the seeds would be arranged in straight lines outward. "Turning" 1.618 times crams the most seeds into that small area.

Getting the most

The sunflower packs in seeds to get the most in a small area. Other plants have Fibonacci patterns in their leaf arrangements. And the number of branches (or roots going down) that develop on a tree follow a sequence of 1, 2, 3, 5, 8, 13... as the best way to capture light.

Animal designs

Shellfish and snails have hard outer shells that spiral outward from a central point. Imagine a rectangle with the longer side 1.618 times longer than the shorter side. And then drawing another rectangle so that the first "longer side" becomes the shorter side. And again, and again. Curving out from corner to corner would produce the exact same spiral.

Some math techniques take humans many years to grasp, but animals use these same tricks instinctively. Math can help us to unlock many secrets of the natural world.

LEONARDO DA VINCI STUDIED THE MOVEMENT OF BIRDS' WINGS WHEN HE WAS TRYING TO INVENT A FLYING MACHINE.

Building the waxworks

It takes a lot of energy to make the wax "shelves" where bees store precious honey. So the honey needs to be stored in the most efficient way, with no gaps between the shelves. Only three shapes, all equilateral, can do that: triangles, squares, and hexagons. And of those, the hexagon has the smallest perimeter (length around its edges)—so it uses the least wax.

Math movement

Scientists believe that ants count their steps and calculate the angle and movement of the Sun to find their way back to a nest. And the way that hundreds of birds fly in a flock, or fish swim in a school, is an example of constant calculation. Those animals manage it through instinct: humans need advanced computers to study the math involved.

Shoals of fish can navigate "in formation"—instantly.

Monkey business

Monkeys can pick the larger of two sets of dots on a computer screen. It seems that they are actually adding up dots to come up with an answer. That skill probably helps them judge food supplies and the number of monkeys in a rival group.

FACT 57

We know what the weather was like—1,000 years ago!

Natural calculations

Most people know that you can judge the age of a tree by counting the rings in its trunk. But those rings—especially the distances between them—tell us much more. Scientists calculate the differences between rings to work out whether the weather in earlier periods was hot or cold, wet or dry. Some trees paint a picture of the weather a thousand years ago.

FACT 58
WE LINK SOME NUMBERS TO THE NATURAL WORLD

A lot of human traditions came from patterns that people saw in the natural world–ranging from the length of a day to the planets in the night sky.

Lucky 7

Human beings naturally use math to find—or create—patterns in the world around them. A day or a year is a natural cycle, so it's obvious that we use them to describe time. But how did we decide on a week of seven days? The answer is found in the Moon's cycle. It takes seven days from New Moon to First Quarter, another seven days to Full Moon, and so on.

How many days in a month?

You may think it would make sense for a month to have 28 days. But it takes about 30 days for the Moon to orbit the Earth (and appear in the same position in the sky). So months are usually about this length.

Guidance from above

The famous Giza pyramids in Egypt are a mathematical "mirror" of the stars in the belt of Orion, a bright constellation*. The three pyramids don't quite form a straight line—instead they line up exactly as the stars above them do. It seems that the ancient Egyptians used geometry (the branch of math devoted to shapes). The angles between the stars of Orion guided them, just as a blueprint guides modern builder.

* A group of stars that seem to form a pattern when we view them from Earth.

FACT 59

Some buildings miss out "unlucky" floors.

Lucky and unlucky numbers

Most people say they are not superstitious, but they may still consider certain numbers "lucky." Other numbers are traditionally seen as bad luck. Tall buildings sometimes miss out "unlucky" floor numbers or rooms. In Western countries, 13 is considered unlucky; in China and parts of Asia it is 4.

PUTTING YOUR SHOES ON IS "COMMUTATIVE"

But getting dressed isn't. You need to put on underwear before you can put on your jeans. Some things can be swapped around, but others rely on sticking to the right order. It's important to know which is which.

Who goes first?

It doesn't matter which shoe you put on first. Similarly, 5 + 7 is the same as 7 + 5. And 5 x 7 is the same as 7 x 5. We say that addition and multiplication are commutative. That means we can change the order around and it makes no difference. Subtraction and division, though, aren't commutative. 20 – 4 is different from 4 – 20 and $^{20}/_4$ leads to a different answer from $^4/_{20}$.

Tying my shoes? It's a simple math problem.

SOME CONVENTIONS ARE USEFUL IN MATH—LIKE WHERE TO PUT COMMAS IN LONG NUMBERS.

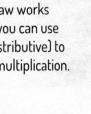

A head start

You can use a similar law, the associative, to group numbers in addition and multiplication: For 3 + 2 + 9, you could do "3 + 2" first, then add 9. Or you could add 3 to "2 + 9." The same law works for multiplication, and you can use yet another law (the distributive) to combine addition and multiplication.

Math problems are a lot easier once you know how to approach them.

Words

For centuries, people worked with what we'd call "word problems," describing what they needed to find out without using number symbols. However, these problems were time consuming. Just think of writing "234 + 1077 + 84" out in words... and then working out the answer without using number symbols.

THE INVENTION OF THE EUROPEAN PRINTING PRESS HELPED PEOPLE AGREE ON HOW MATH PROBLEMS SHOULD BE PRESENTED AND SOLVED.

Signs of the times

Some of the short-cuts and laws that we use to simplify calculations really only work with number symbols. And it's not just symbols for numbers that make life easier. Many of our familiar symbols, such as +, -, x, and = all developed as ways to calculate more quickly.

FACT 61

The plus sign (+) is a simplified version of the Roman word "et" meaning "and."

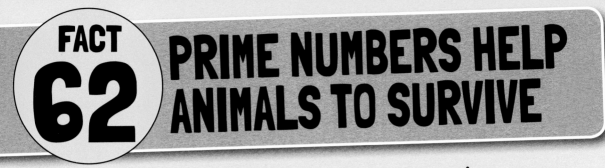

FACT 62 PRIME NUMBERS HELP ANIMALS TO SURVIVE

Prime numbers can only be divided by themselves, or one. And mathematicians aren't the only ones interested in them. Insects have entire life cycles based on prime numbers.

WHEN PERIODIC CICADAS HATCH, THEY REALLY ARRIVE IN NUMBERS—SOMETIMES 3.5 MILLION IN EACH HECTARE OF LAND.

Prime-time arrivals

All insects hatch into a larvae before emerging as adults—and usually the insects become adults at the same time every year. But periodical cicadas of eastern North America have a much longer gap between each new wave. These locust-like insects emerge either every 13 or 17 years. It's those "periods" of 13 or 17 years that give the insects their name. And it's not a coincidence that 13 and 17 are both prime numbers!

Boom and bust

Having a prime-number gap between appearances gives the cicada a real advantage. And it is all down to the population cycle of its predators. Most animals have years when their population is larger and years when it is smaller. It depends on the amount of food available and how many predators are around.

Cicada with 12-year life cycle

predator with 2-year life cycle:
overlap in years 12, 24, 36, 48, and 60

predator with 3-year life cycle:
overlap in years 12, 24, 36, 48, and 60

Cicada with 13-year life cycle

predator with 2-year life cycle:
overlap in years 26 and 52

predator with 3-year life cycle:
overlap in years 39

Avoiding the enemy

Cicadas want to avoid emerging during years when there are many predators. A prime number life cycle is the best way of doing that. It gives the cicada the best chance of emerging in a year when its predators' populations are low. Just look at how often a cicada with a 12-year life cycle coincides with its predators compared to a 13-year cicada. You won't be surprised to hear that there are no 12-year cicadas!

FACT 63

The fiddler crab's claw gets stronger every 29.5 days.

Lunar cycles

Male fiddler crabs try to attract mates with their strong snapping claw. But females only want to mate at the full moon or the new moon. This ensures their babies emerge at high tides, when the strong ocean currents will sweep them far away and give them the best chance of survival. So the male crabs put on their best displays once a month. Snap! Snap!

YOU CAN KEEP SECRETS SECRET WITH MATH

Numbers and letters are both symbols that can be arranged in millions of ways. So when people want to hide messages, they often use math to make their code harder to break.

Number jumble

Codemakers try to stump people who shouldn't see a message. They use basic numerals to stand for the 26 letters of the alphabet. A simple code might chage the letter "A" to the number 1 and change "Z" to 26. But things can get much more complicated than that!

Keep answers secret

Governments need to keep track of their secret codes, as well as the solutions. That sort of top-secret information is contained in codebooks. These collections were once written down by hand in real books, kept in locked briefcases fastened to secret agents' wrists. Today, "codebooks" are usually special computer files.

Carrying codebooks was often a risky business for spies.

HIDING MESSAGES IN SECRET CODES IS CALLED ENCRYPTION. SOLVING THE CODES IS CALLED DECRYPTION.

Hidden messages

Prime numbers are an excellent way to code messages, and computers use very large prime numbers to send information securely. This system relies on the fact that it is very easy to multiply two large prime numbers together, but almost impossible to work out what the prime numbers are by looking at the answer.

Useful practise

The skills developed from working with codes helps people in other areas of math. In algebra, you need to switch back and forth between numbers, letters, and other symbols. Many math problems are easier to solve if you substitute letters for numbers.

CODEBREAKERS HELPED WIN A WAR... SECRETLY!

Imagine trying to break a code that had 159 million, million possible solutions, and that your country would be invaded if you failed. Well, it really happened...

Math minds to the rescue

Some of the brightest math experts in Poland and Great Britain took on a mighty challenge for the Allies during World War II. They worked to unscramble the complicated code system that the Nazis used for their communications. The task seemed impossible. Enigma, the machine that produced the system, changed typed letters into code, and then those letters into code, and then those letters into code. And the method changed all the time!

AN ENIGMA IS SOMETHING THAT IS MYSTERIOUS AND PUZZLING.

Race against time

Breaking the code meant that the Allies could find out how and where the Nazis prepared for an attack from Britain. That called for more math to work out whether Allied ships would land enough soldiers before Nazi weapons and soldiers could be sent to drive them back.

Codebreakers did more to prevent invasion than gun bunkers.

Did the code really say we have to march all day?

Important calculations

Alan Turing, a leading codebreaker in World War II, invented one of the first modern computers to break the Enigma code. It used probability—the branch of math looking at how likely things are to happen—to eliminate millions of unlikely solutions. The codebreakers could then concentrate on what was left, which still called for the highest math skills. By late 1941 they had created a method that could break the Enigma code on most days.

A long history

Using coded messages goes back much further than the 20th century. It's well known that the famous Roman soldier and leader Julius Caesar sent messages to soldiers in code. His system, called the Caesar Shift, originally used just letters, shifting them a few places along the alphabet. The code soon developed to use numbers in place of letters.

MATH CODES SAVE PEOPLE'S LIVES

What links your bike with top-secret "launch buttons" for long-range missiles? The answer is codes, which use math to help stop the wrong people from using them.

Safety in numbers

Security sometimes means just a good lock and key. But some locks can be "picked" (opened with special tools) and keys can be copied, so the best keys are the ones that you keep in your head. That means using codes to remember your bike lock combination or PIN. You can combine math skills with obvious numbers such as birthdays to create your own code.

ABOUT 11 PERCENT OF PEOPLE CHOOSE "1234" AS THEIR FOUR-DIGIT PIN.

High security

Four-digit codes, like the ones for PINs and bike locks, are pretty easy to create—and crack. For really serious protection, the sort that banks and the military need, you need to become far more complicated and mathematical. These codes add many extra layers of difficulty, and usually have timers to stop illegal attempts midway through.

US PRESIDENTS USED TO CARRY A DAILY-CHANGING CARD GIVING THE NUCLEAR CODE. THEY MEMORIZED THE POSITION OF THE ACCURATE CODE, HIDDEN AMONG THE FAKES.

Hold your fire!

It's bad if someone cracks the code on your bike lock, but it's not the end of the world. Armed forces, though, worry that code-cracking could launch missiles that could destroy whole cities. Their launch codes rely on advanced math to prevent the wrong people from working them out.

FACT 67

From 1962 to 1977, the US "code" to launch nuclear missiles was said to be simply "00000000."

Too many codes?

What if a country was under direct attack, and a weapons officer couldn't work out the math for the codeword? Some codes, before information could be stored on computers, were worryingly simple—and didn't need any math to figure out! Now people need a code for the code for the code.

85

DECIMALS HELP YOU CHOOSE WHAT TO READ

Think of how you could arrange books about different subjects in a library. Alphabetically, so that "bugs" would be next to "buttons"? No, the best way is to use numbers instead.

> Hmmm... this feels like a 744.76 to me.

THE DEWEY DECIMAL SYSTEM IS USED IN MORE THAN 135 COUNTIRES.

Find the right number

You wouldn't expect to walk into a library and be able to find books on, say, Egypt's pyramids right away. But you would if you knew that the books on ancient Egypt all have a code beginning with "932." And once you'd found that section, you'd see that it is subdivided into 932.2, 932.8 and so on. The numbers after the decimal point can group subjects further. You'd also know that books on these subjects would have the same numbering in other libraries.

Bits of the whole

Those numbers on the library books are the Dewey Decimal System. Decimals, like fractions, express relationships. They convert the relationship into tenths, written after a period (called a decimal point). So 0.5 is the same as five tenths, or $^5/_{10}$. And 0.8 is the same as eight tenths, or $^8/_{10}$. It's a neat system, tying in with our base 10 math.

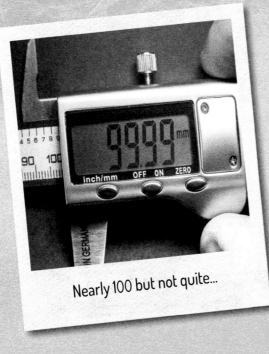

Nearly 100 but not quite...

How many places?

Some fractions turn easily into decimals. The easiest are "tenths," because the job's already done, and you could just write 0.5 or 0.8. Some decimals need two or more numbers after the decimal point: ¼, for example, is 0.25. Others are trickier, going on and on like the millions of places for pi.

FACT 69

Some decimals go on and on and on and never end.

Photo finish

Decimals help us express very precise results. Most professional races are timed to two decimal places—hundredths of a second—but some races are close enough to need three decimal places—thousandths of a second.

BRITISH RACING DRIVER KRISTIAN KOLBY WON THE 2005 KANSAS INDY LIGHTS RACE BY JUST 0.001 OF A SECOND.

THERE'S ZERO... THEN THERE'S ABSOLUTE ZERO

If your thermometer reads "zero" then you know it's cold. But that "zero" might be describing a much colder temperature if your thermometer is from another country... or a science lab.

Measuring the world

The Fahrenheit temperature scale, used in the United States, sets its zero 32 degrees colder than the freezing point of water. And using the Fahrenheit scale, water boils at 212 degrees. Most other parts of the world use Celsius to measure heat and cold. Using the Celsius scale, water freezes at zero degrees and boils at 100 degrees. So a temperature of zero is much colder in New York than in London.

A BANANA EXPOSED TO ABSOLUTE ZERO FREEZES HARD ENOUGH TO BE USED AS A HAMMER.

Down to absolute zero

Using water as the starting point (zero) of a temperature makes sense. Most people have seen water freeze and boil. But many scientists use yet another scale, the Kelvin scale. The gaps between degrees are the same as in Celsius, but the scale starts at absolute zero and goes up from there. Absolute zero is the temperature where all motion stops, even in the smallest atoms.

Getting negative

The real world is the best way to learn about some difficult math ideas. Some people have a hard time understanding negative numbers, which begin at zero and go "the wrong way." But a temperature of "six below zero" is just another way of saying "negative six."

You don't need to be a math whizz to feel wind chill.

FACT 71

Adding in wind chill explains why you feel colder than the thermometer suggests.

Wind chill

A thermometer accurately measures the temperature of the air, but we also lose heat when it's windy. Scientists have found a method, called wind chill, to describe how cold we feel in certain weather. They combine wind speed with temperature to calculate wind chill. A very windy 25-degree day could have a wind chill of -5 degrees and feel colder than a 20-degree day with no wind.

A CENT CAN "DOUBLE" TO MILLIONS IN WEEKS

Imagine a visitor to the USA has one cent, and finds a way to double the money she has every day. At first the amounts are small, but watch what happens when numbers meet the "power of powers."

Powering ahead

The increase is based on the power of 2. By the second day, the single cent has become two, or "2 to the power of 1" (2 multiplied by itself once). By the 31st day, it has reached "2 to the power of 30": 1,073,741,824 cents, or $10,737,418.24. This rapid increase is an example of exponential growth: You multiply a number by something to get the next one.

EXPONENTIAL GROWTH IS MUCH MORE RAPID THAN LINEAR GROWTH, WHERE THE SAME AMOUNT IS ADDED EACH TIME.

Letters can represent numbers—and so even letters can have exponents.

Writing shortcut

A small number above and to the right of another number is called an exponent. It tells us the number of times the lower number is multiplied by itself (or "raised to that power"). So 8^4 is a quick way of writing 8x8x8x8, or "8 raised to the power of four."

RAISING TO THE POWER OF TWO IS ALSO CALLED "SQUARING"; "CUBING" DESCRIBES RAISING TO THE POWER OF THREE.

It's a good thing!

Exponential growth can be helpful. Banks pay savers interest on their money each year. It's a percentage of the savings, including the interest that's already been added. That's called compound interest.

FACT 73

An Australian farmer imported 24 English rabbits in 1859. Within six years, the rabbit population had multiplied to 22 million.

It's a bad thing!

Exponential growth can also multiply problems. Australia had no native rabbits until people brought them in. The rabbit population grew exponentially. Within a few years, rabbits were out of control and damaging farms across the country.

DOCTORS FIGHT EPIDEMICS WITH MATH

Many diseases spread from one person to many, and then to many more. Knowing how many people are at risk, and how fast a disease spreads, helps doctors to fight back.

Tracking disease

If someone sneezes on a crowded bus, people nearby can catch the illness. Ten or more people might become ill. And if each of them passes it on to others, then the disease can spread quickly. This rapid spread follows an exponential pattern (see pages 90-91). Medical experts can use math to prepare for the outbreak.

AN "EPIDEMIC" IS WHEN MANY PEOPLE IN ONE AREA COME DOWN WITH A DISEASE. IT BECOMES A "PANDEMIC" IF IT SPREADS FROM COUNTRY TO COUNTRY.

Medical math

Exponential growth of an illness calls for quick thinking. How many hospital beds will be needed? Will there be enough medicine to cope? That's dealing with the outbreak. Slowing or stopping the spread of infection also calls for math—how many infected people need to be isolated and how many healthy people need to be vaccinated to stop the spread.

Vaccination health

If enough people are vaccinated against a disease, then the disease does not spread far. High vaccination rates protect people who cannot be vaccinated: for example, newborn babies or those with very weak immune systems.

Early tracking of diseases can prevent epidemics.

FACT 75

If you could fold a sheet of newspaper 25 times, the sheet would be taller than the Eiffel Tower.

Hard to grasp

Exponential growth is some of the most interesting, and most misunderstood, bits of math. Even the simplest exponential growth—increasing by the power of two—can surprise us. It's easy to forget that folding something doubles its thickness exponentially, so that it "doubles the doubled double" and so on.

MATH CAN PREDICT THE COURSE OF HURRICANES

These destructive storms once struck without warning, making their effect even deadlier. But math can now help predict the way in which hurricanes behave—offering people a chance to escape.

Judging the risks

You've probably heard weather reports talking about a 30 percent chance of rain or a 10 percent chance of snow. Those predictions are based on probability, the branch of mathematics that studies how likely things are to happen. A 30 percent chance of showers tomorrow tells you whether to pack an umbrella. But a 50 percent chance of a serious storm such as a hurricane helps you make far more important plans.

SEVERE STORMS HAVE DIFFERENT NAMES IN DIFFERENT PLACES: "HURRICANES" IN NORTH AND SOUTH AMERICA, "TYPHOONS" IN THE WESTERN PACIFIC AND "CYCLONES" IN THE INDIAN OCEAN.

Weather planes fly through and above storm centers to provide data.

Gathering information

Probability predicts how often an event takes place if another event is repeated. If you flipped a coin 100 times (repeating one event), you would predict that it would land on heads 50 times giving it a probability of ½. Scientists examine certain weather conditions repeatedly. They note how often they lead to other events such as hurricanes taking place. That probability helps them predict how often—and where—hurricanes might form.

Collision course?

A 10 percent chance of rain is the same as a one-in-ten (¹⁄₁₀) chance that it will rain. Some natural events, though, have a much smaller probability, even though the event itself is far scarier. Scientists believe that a huge meteorite crashed into Earth 65 million years ago, destroying plants and animals (including dinosaurs). The probability that another will strike the Earth in the next 50 years? About one in 18 million (¹⁄₁₈,₀₀₀,₀₀₀).

Just like clockwork

Some natural events, such as earthquakes, are almost impossible to predict using probability. Others have a predicatable schedule. Tourists can almost set their watches by America's "Old Faithful" geyser in Yellowstone National Park.

FACT 77 INSURANCE COMPANIES LOVE GAMBLING

Well, it's not real gambling like betting on horse races or playing poker. But their success does depend on judging whether certain events will occur in the future. It's all down to probability.

SEVERAL COMPANIES OFFER PEOPLE THE CHANCE TO INSURE AGAINST THE RISK OF BEING CAPTURED BY ALIENS.

Peace of mind

Insurance companies offer the chance to guard against the cost of replacing a car. Customers pay an amount each year, and if the car is in a serious accident, the insurance company pays the full cost of replacing it. The company studies how likely it is that it will need to "pay out." This tells them how much to charge customers for insuring their car.

Payout for a washout

People can insure many things, from cell phones to expensive paintings. They can also insure events. Organizers of outdoor concerts, for example, can take out insurance so that they can refund ticket prices if rain cancels the event. The insurance company bases its charge on the probability of bad weather on the day. It would charge more if the concert is held somewhere that sees a lot of rain.

An expensive smile

Probability can crop up in unusual ways for insurance companies. They will sometimes agree to pay millions if injury or accident prevents a musician or actor from performing. Sports stars can have their arms or legs insured, pianists can insure their fingers and some people even insure their hair. Actress America Ferrera (right) has her smile insured for $10 million.

FACT 78 You can find true love through a computer program.

Love at first byte

Some companies use probability to help people find life partners. Interested customers enter lots of information about their interests and activities into the company's computer system. The computer then examines its information to provide a match from its store of other customer's information. The company's success depends on how well it has judged the probability to find a successful match.

TWO PEOPLE IN A CLASS SHARE A BIRTHDAY

There's really a "probably" in there: two people probably share a birthday. Math tells us that in any room of 23 people, it's more likely than not that two people were born on the same day.

Number crunching

"More likely than not" means that there's a better than 50 percent chance that two people will share a birthday. In fact, it's a 50.05 percent chance, but it takes a lot of detailed calculation to reach that answer. The hard part is knowing where to start. Remember: It's not just you finding a match from 22 other people, it's everyone. That means that there are 253 pairs that might give a match.

AN OCTOPUS KNOWN AS PAUL CORRECTLY PREDICTED THE OUTCOME OF GERMANY'S SIX WORLD CUP SOCCER MATCHES IN 2010... COMPLETELY BY CHANCE!

Important guidance

Many examples of probability, like the shared birthdays, seem hard to believe. But this branch of math isn't just looking at things that are likely to happen. It calculates what could happen. That ability to calculate possibilities is very important. It helps us build up stocks of medicine, keep machinery safe and work out how much money to set aside for all sorts of emergencies.

Family predictions

Some of the most familiar examples of probability are all around you. Genetics, the study of what parents pass on to their children, uses probability to make some general predictions. What is the chance you will have a left-handed child? Genetics tell us it's one in 10 if both parents are right-handed, about three in 10 if both parents are left-handed.

In the past, left-handers were forced to write with their right hand.

FACT
80
You can win at rock-paper-scissors without being a mind reader.

Playground probability

People can combine the math skills of probability with psychology (the study of how people behave) to make some surprising predictions. Even familiar games of "chance" (luck) can be studied to gain an advantage. For example, a winner of rock-paper-scissors tends to use the same choice in the next go, while the loser moves to the next choice.

Democracy means choosing our leaders by voting for them. That means that they are "the people's choice." But sometimes we simply choose the person who seems most likely to win.

An accurate reflection...

The boundary between math (probability) and psychology can really become blurred at election time. People naturally want to learn more about the candidates, and voters are often polled (questioned) about who they are likely to vote for. Political experts study these polls and then use probability to judge the chances of each candidate.

...or maybe a prediction?

But some voters are affected by the results of the polls and vote differently. They might not bother to vote if their candidate seems likely to lose, or they could switch their vote to the likely winner, if one candidate is doing surprisingly well.

THE WORLD'S LARGEST DEMOCRACY IS INDIA, WITH MORE THAN 800 MILLION VOTERS.

Getting things wrong

Political parties and news broadcasting companies spend millions during elections to get an accurate prediction of the outcome. Sometimes the results are remarkably accurate. But although the methods call for intense math calculations, it's human beings who do the actual voting. People can be unpredictable. Sometimes, what's expected to be a crushing defeat for one party can turn into a stunning victory as the real results come in.

Informed choice

Of course, political parties and candidates don't just sit around and wait for probability to run its course. In the weeks before an election, they run advertising to persuade voters—and to increase the probability of their victory. That, in turn, calls for the close study of ads that succeeded in the past.

All advertisements aim to sway public opinion in some way.

FACT 82
It's better to answer "true" to a true/false question if you don't know the answer.

Educated guess

It's not just political experts who make predictions based on studying earlier answers. People have found that the answer to more than half of true/false questions is "true," for lots of reasons—mainly because it's hard to think of believable, but wrong, answers. That's why probability says that we should answer "true" if we're not sure.

ONE CAT HAD THREE LIVES!

Some stories seem like nonsense but turn out to be almost true. At the same time, there are "sensible" math ideas that are way off target. What's going on?

Soft landing

An old saying has it that cats have nine lives. It might seem like that when we see how cats can leap from great heights and land unhurt. But of course cats do just have one life, which lasts on average 12 years. The cat with the longest-known life (38 years) lived more than three times that long. So you could say this cat lived three lives... but would that be good math?

KNOWING WHICH NUMBERS WERE DRAWN IN THE PAST HAS NO EFFECT ON YOUR CHANCES OF WINNING A LOTTERY.

The full story

Math figures can be accurate... but do you have the whole story? You might be told there are half a million pieces of space "trash," such as bits of old satellites, that will soon fall to Earth. Scared? It sounds like a big number, so you might feel there is a real risk of being hit. But most of these bits will burn up in the atmosphere: the chance of one hitting you is one in a billion!

Working our way up

One way in which mathematicians try to make sure their data is accurate is by using extrapolations. If we know exact figures for something small (like the number of pupils in a class with colds) we can then extrapolate—estimate that the same proportion of people in a town might be fighting colds.

SCIENTISTS MONITOR SPACE "DEBRIS" THAT MIGHT COME NEAR THE INTERNATIONAL SPACE STATION. THEY CHANGE ITS COURSE IF THE DEBRIS IS LARGER THAN 2 INCHES (5 CM).

Guessing saves lives

Extrapolating information can be very useful. For example, someone with an heart problems may be asked to wear an ECG device for 24 hours to record their heartbeat. This "snapshot" of the heart can be used by doctors to diagnose a problem and find a suitable treatment.

Estimating accurately is a vital skill in medicine—and life.

LEARNING MUSIC CAN HELP YOUR MATH

Blasting out a tune on a trumpet or a bouncing beat on a bass guitar might seem miles away from mastering math. But some strong connections link these skills.

A musical head start

Music is all about patterns, rhythms, and beats. And one of the most basic of all math skills—counting—lies at the heart of understanding how a piece of music should be played. Even pitch (how high or low a note sounds) can be described using math. Reading music and learning to play an instrument help you understand these real-life uses of math.

SOME PEOPLE LEARN TO READ MUSIC AT THE SAME TIME AS LEARNING TO READ WORDS.

The brain game

When you're exposed to music—either listening or playing—parts of your brain become more active. And like muscles after you have regular exercise, those bits of the brain begin to work better and even to get a bit bigger. The cortex, or part of the brain dealing with "higher thought" (like math), is one of the winners.

Two friends working hard to boost their brainpower.

COMPUTERS CAN USE MATH TO ADJUST A SINGER'S VOICE TO MAKE THEM SING "IN TUNE."

Beat it

Musicians know the beat of a piece of music because of numbers written on their music. Those numbers, called time signatures, look like fractions but they're really about counting. And they're another way that young musicians can get the "feel" of math topics, making them easier to understand in the classroom.

Putting it all together

Lots of math involves using symbols to represent other things. Some people find the jump from "plain numbers" to "symbols" scary when they come across them at school. Musicians don't have so much trouble. After all, they're used to working with symbols and numbers, helping them to work out when to play, how fast, how softly or loudly... not to mention which note!

DANCE STEPS DEPEND ON MATH

The pattern and timing of dance steps are dictated by rhythm, a combination of math and time. So it's hardly surprising that dance's partner, music, is also in step with math.

Best foot forward

A dance teacher will call out "1-2-3, 1-2-3, 1-2-3" in time with the music as she teaches people the waltz. That's because waltz music always follows the same three-beat rhythm. Other dances, such as polkas, salsa, and disco, follow special rhythms that mark them out too. Tap dancing involves playing around with the music's rhythm or even creating a different rhythm.

SOME SCHOOLS USE DANCE TO TEACH CHILDREN GEOMETRY.

Learning through dance

Dance can be a good way to teach people about math. Think about how children learn to count, or to form counting patterns, as they play with a jump rope. The "steps" of jumping make those counting simple rhythms easy to feel, and understand. More complicated dance rhythms can help people "feel" their way into more advanced math ideas, such as sets.

This ballet dancer's arabesque forms an 180-degree angle.

A SIMPLE SQUARE DANCE DEMONSTRATES EIGHT TYPES OF SYMMETRY—FOUR ROTATION SYMMETRIES AND FOUR REFLECTIVE.

Dance geometry

Many types of dance use familiar geometric shapes as ideals for the dancers. Ballet has a number of classical positions that call for dancers to create right angles, circles, or straight lines. Hip-hop dancing also calls for precise creation of angles and other geometric shapes.

Shifting patterns

It's not just the mix of music rhythm and movement that links dance with math. The actual performance of a dance can produce shifting patterns and geometric shapes. Many types of dance send their performers through steps and movements that produce constantly changing triangles, pentagons, circles, and lines.

SUDOKUS WERE INSPIRED BY TURTLES

The modern form of sudoku puzzle was invented in 1979, but similar number puzzles have been known for centuries. Their history can be traced back to ancient legends about how a turtle saved a village.

THERE ARE 5,472,730,538 POSSIBLE SUDOKU PUZZLES.

2	7	6	→15
9	5	1	→15
4	3	8	→15

↓ 15 ↓ 15 ↓ 15 ↘ 15

Flood protection

The roots of today's sudokus go back to the "number squares" of ancient China and India. These were patterns with nine squares, and the solution used numbers 1 to 9 once so that every row, column and diagonal added up to 15. Legend has it that Chinese villagers saw such a number square on a turtle's shell, and the "15" was the number of sacrifices they needed to make to protect their village against floods.

"No math needed"?

Newspapers will often print "no math needed" next to that day's sudoku puzzles. What they really mean is that no arithmetic is needed. You don't have to add, subtract, multiply, or divide. But the difficulty—and pleasure—of solving a sudoku is really all about math, particularly finding and completing patterns without repeating any symbols.

Prescription: one sudoku puzzle to be taken daily.

AN INDIAN PUZZLE SETTER HAS DESIGNED A SUDOKU WITH 100 ROWS, 100 COLUMNS, AND 100 GRIDS.

Puzzle help

Just as exercising helps people become and stay fit, doing "pattern puzzles" such as sudokus exercises the brain. People get better at solving them with practice. Doctors also use these puzzles to help patients recover from conditions that affect the brain.

FACT 87

If you look at any dice you will see that the opposite sides always add up to 7.

Everyday patterns

Many everyday patterns become so familiar to us that our minds use math to complete them, even if we only see a part. The pattern could be as different as a dartboard is from a computer keyboard, but we use similar skills to understand them. That same ability to work out "what goes where" is what we use to solve sudoku puzzles.

YOU CAN WIN MORE POINTS BUT STILL LOSE IN TENNIS

The scoring in tennis can lead to some odd results. And it's not just sports and games that seem to break the rules of mathematics... or common sense.

Settling scores

It's simple to work out the winner in most sports. The player or team that scores the most points wins, whether they're playing football, basketball, or baseball. But a tennis match is broken down into sets and games... and then points. Both players try to win each point, but those points don't count directly toward overall victory. So, in a match scored 1-6, 7-5, 7-5, the winner would have won one fewer game than the loser (15 compared to 16).

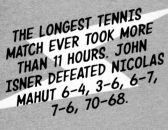

THE LONGEST TENNIS MATCH EVER TOOK MORE THAN 11 HOURS. JOHN ISNER DEFEATED NICOLAS MAHUT 6-4, 3-6, 6-7, 7-6, 70-68.

Quick calculations

Sports and games often call for math skills. Bridge and poker players keep track of which cards have been played to work out what remains. They then use probability to guess what is likely to happen next.

A bridge player calculates the best way to score points.

THE FEWEST NUMBER OF DARTS THAT CAN BE THROWN TO WIN A GAME IS NINE. YOU NEED TO HIT TRIPLE 20 SIX TIMES, THEN TRIPLE 17, TRIPLE 18, AND DOUBLE 18.

Bullseye

Darts players need to be good at subtraction as well as accurate throwing. The dartboard is divided into numbered sections, and if you hit a number it is taken off your score. You are aiming to get from 501 points to zero. You need to subtract quickly to work out your new score, and decide which number is best to aim at.

Majority rules?

Many countries decide their government by counting the votes separately in different areas. The political party with the most of these smaller victories wins overall. But it might have won by just a handful of votes in each of its "victories," and had hardly any votes in the others. Some United States presidents, including President George W. Bush, have been elected with fewer votes than their opponents.

FACT 89

A SHARK'S SENSE OF SMELL IS ONE IN A MILLION

A shark's sense of smell is so acute that it can detect one part blood within a million parts of water. That leads to a ratio of 1:1,000,000.

Scary numbers

A ratio is a way of comparing two numbers of a similar kind. This ratio 1:1,000,000 is comparing two liquids—blood and seawater. The most "mathematical" way to express a ratio is with numerals (such as 1:1,000,000 for blood and seawater). But sometimes it's easier for people to understand— or get scared by—ratios if we express them differently. One million gallons of water is quite hard to picture, but you could express the ratio using something familiar, such as "sharks can detect half a gallon of blood in an Olympic-sized swimming pool."

RATIOS CAN BE REDUCED, JUST LIKE FRACTIONS. A RATIO OF 12:48 IS THE SAME AS 6:24, 3:12, 2:8 OR 1:4.

All in the mix

We come across ratios all the time, even if we don't recognize them. At the supermarket we compare the price-per-pound of products to decide on the best deal. At school we might tally up the number of left- and right-handed students. If, for example, there are three left-handers and 27 right-handers, then the ratio is 3:27.

Fair rate of pay

Ratios also play a part in the ways that people are rewarded for their work. People are often paid a certain amount per hour or week. These ratios are called hourly or weekly rates. And companies usually provide holidays, often considered as a number of days per year—the more days the better!

FACT 90

A cyclist must pick the right ratio to go uphill.

What goes up....

Bicycle gears operate as ratios. If you're climbing a hill, you use a small gear (with fewer teeth) by the pedals and a big gear (with lots of teeth) at the back. The number of teeth might have a ratio of 11:44. It's pretty easy to push the bike a quarter of a rear-wheel rotation, which is how far one pedal-gear rotation pushes the rear gear. But it doesn't get you as far as the (more tiring) 22:44 combination.

TWO HUNDRED THOUSAND TONS OF METAL CAN FLOAT

A huge ship made of steel and weighing more than 200,000 tons can float as easily as a cork. But a steel spoon will sink. Where does math come into it?

Floating ratios

Ratios—that's where. Things float when they are less dense than the fluid surrounding them. And density is all about a specific ratio: mass to volume (or the weight of an object compared to the space it fills). The volume of the ship includes its spaces, which weigh very little. And that lowers its density. The spoon has a small mass, but a tiny volume.

THE SEAWISE GIANT, THE LARGEST SHIP EVER BUILT, WEIGHED 724,239 TONS.

Over the edge?

Buoyancy, the force that keeps things floating, depends on how much water an object displaces, or pushes away. You can see that displacement when you get in the bath and the water rises... and sometimes spills out. The buoyancy force equals the weight of the water that's been displaced.

Vela

SIRIUS STAR

Up and down

If a supertanker can float because the ratio of its mass and volume works, then what about a submarine? Again, it's about ratios, but ones that can be adjusted. A sub that's climbing or on the surface has tubes filled with air. If it needs to dive, the crew pumps water into those tubes, increasing the mass in the ratio.

I'll just lean against this chair...

Other ratios

Ratios are often the best way to prepare a government's "report card." Citizens expect their governments to raise some ratios, such as "teachers:pupils in schools" or "doctors:1,000 people in a country." Other ratios, such as "crimes:10,000 people," should be reduced if a government wants to remain in power.

FACT 92 Gravity is a weak force, even on Earth. We can overcome it just by standing up!

May the force be with you

All objects create gravity, but the amount depends on the mass of the object. Most objects create only a very tiny amount of gravity, but the mass of the Earth is huge and we can certainly feel the gravity created by our planet! The Moon has one sixth of the Earth's mass. That means the ratio of its gravity compared to Earth's is 1:6. Seen another way, it tells us that moving objects can go six times further on the Moon than on Earth before gravity pulls them down.

RATIOS HELP YOU COOK FOR FRIENDS

Recipes give you the quantities of the ingredients. But what happens if you want to cook more or less than the amount suggested? You need to use ratios to help you.

IN 2015, SPANISH BAKERS USED MORE THAN 660 LB. (300 KG) OF DOUGH TO PRODUCE A GIANT LOAF OF BREAD. IT TOOK 3 HOURS TO BAKE.

The right mix

Some quick calculations can save the day if extra dinner guests arrive. You had worked out how much of each ingredient you needed to serve six. Now you're going to feed twelve. That's a ratio — 6:12. And since, like fractions, ratios can reduce... you get 1:2. So you will need to double all of the original ingredients of your sauce to get that special flavor. Oh, and don't forget to double the amount of pasta, too!

The volume of a bread roll is "nothing" when I've eaten it!

Bread rolls need less time to cook than a large loaf of bread.

But take care

You need to take care with ratios. You can double the size of your bread dough, but you can't just double the cooking time. That's because—like any 3-D shape—the voume increases at a faster rate than the surface area. Your bread would be burned on the outside and raw in the middle! Better bake two loaves of the original size.

Spotting bargains

You can work with ratios to find out if you're looking at a bargain on a supermarket shelf or a magazine advertisement. "Buy two, get one free" deals are telling you that you get three but pay for two. That's a simple 3:2 ratio. A cell phone plan offering a certain price per 100 texts might seem more expensive than one charging per single text... until you do the calculation.

FACT
94

Cooking is like following a math formula.

Experiments to eat

A good cook is a good mathematician. It's all about following instructions in the right order. And of course once you understand what to do you will be able to repeat the formula for delicious results every time!

YOU CAN PRINT A GOLF BALL WITH 1s AND 0s

We use computers for our homework, printing photos, or producing party invitations. But the latest programs and printers go much further—instructing computers to "print" solid objects.

The new dimension

Computers use code to transfer information from a file to a printer. Like just about everything to do with computers, this exchange operates in a binary (base 2) system. The result is a series of bursts of ink, then pauses, to create images or words. When you print something at home, the words and pictures are in two dimensions — length and width. 3-D printers have a third dimension, depth.

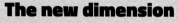

Adding depth

Computer models can also add depth (the third dimension) to an object. These 3-D files go one step further—communicating with a printer that actually produces the object. The printer views it as a series of slices, like a pile of pancakes. Its nozzle squirts out liquid plastic (or other material that can harden) layer by layer to re-create the computer model in real life.

FACT 96 You can create a shape with only one side.

Adding a twist

Mathematicians are fascinated by strange shapes. Take a strip of paper and give it a half-twist, then tape the ends together. You've created a Mobius strip, which upsets our view of geometry. If you draw a line on the outside edge all the way around you'll find that there's no inside or outside edge—just one. Looking at what happens to shapes as they bend, stretch, and twist is called topology.

What do you keep in your Klein bottle?

Adding a twist

The Mobius strip is, strictly speaking, a two-dimensional shape, but mathematicians have created a 3-D shape with only a single edge. This is called the Klein bottle. This shape can exist in real life, although it takes a skilled glassblower to make one! The Science Museum in London, UK, has many examples of Klein bottles, each slightly different.

HUMANS HAVE LIVED JUST OVER A MINUTE

One of the most rewarding branches of math is statistics, which deals with ways of presenting complicated ideas in simple terms. But "just over a minute"—can that be right?

Earth's 24-hour clock

A statistician (someone who works with statistics) can interpret numbers. We know that the Earth is about 4.5 billion years old, and the first humans emerged about 2.5 million years ago. Those are both big numbers, but they don't get across how "young" humans are. If the entire history of Earth were squeezed into 24 hours, then humans would only emerge after 23 hours, 58 minutes and 48 seconds later. That's just before midnight.

IF YOU SHOW THE HISTORY OF THE EARTH ON A 24-HOUR CLOCK, THEN DINOSAURS APPEARERD ABOUT 10.56 PM.

midnight

10.56 pm: dinosaurs evolve

9 pm: jellyfish evolve

6 pm

3 am: meteors hit the Earth

6 am

6 am: first life on Earth

3 pm: algae evolve

noon

Trouble brewing?

Statistics can be used to predict what will happen in the future. They can give a good idea of the "direction" of a trend, and how fast it is happening. This is essential in planning for the future.

Trouble brewing?

One area where statistics are valuable is the subject of population growth. We need to be able to feed and house ourselves. The world's population reached 1 billion in 1804. It took another 123 years to add another billion. But the jump from 6 billion to 7 billion (reached in 2011) was just 12 years. What will happen in the future?

Population clock

Mathematicians can't witness every birth and death on the planet, so they calculate the future based on up-to-date information from every country. They can plug those figures into a "population clock," which makes constant estimates. It shows the world population increasing by about 170,000 every day.

FACT 98

About 6 percent of all the people who ever lived are alive today.

Big cities are already feeling the effects of overcrowding.

Predictions based on math are bound to be true, right? Well, not always. Mathematicians are aware that in the real world, all data has built-in mistakes.

Margin of error

The best way to predict an election winner would be to ask every voter beforehand. That's impossible, so you choose a sample—a smaller group that matches the overall population. Math experts then work out two things: first, which party is likely to win the election and second, the "margin of error." This calculates how representative the sample is, and so how likely it is that the sample group can predict the result.

The bigger the better

To be representative, a sample group must match the general population. Statisticians must work out how to ensure a "match." They try to ensure their sample is representative in terms of age, sex, location, education, and wealth. Usually, the larger the sample the more representative it is.

COMPANIES SOMETIMES LOSE MILLIONS BY MISCALCULATING PUBLIC OPINION.

Market research

Sample groups are also used by companies to plan new products and advertisements. This is called market research. However, sometimes market research gets things very wrong. The Ford Motor Company introduced a new model, the Edsel, in 1958. It had tested people's likes and dislikes in a car to come up with the design. But the car proved unpopular and production stopped two years later.

The same statistics can be presented in different ways.

FACT **100** Statistics can use numbers to trick people.

Tricked by numbers?

Statistics can be misleading. It's usually not the numbers that are false. Instead it's the way in which they're presented. This could be something like not starting a graph at zero to make differences look bigger, or it could be the wording. A "100 percent increase in injuries in one year" might simply mean that one person (out of 12,000) was injured one year and two people were injured the next.

We're used to thinking of the world in three dimensions. But mathematicians consider time to be a fourth dimension. Could we ever learn to manipulate time itself... and maybe travel back to the past?

Time out

Today, science and math have taken journeys into places that no one could imagine just a century or so ago. Now mathematicians studying geometry are looking at the dimension of time. We are familiar with an object's length, width, and depth—so can we study an object in time?

SOME MATH THEORIES IMAGINE EIGHT, TEN, OR MORE THAN TWENTY DIMENSIONS.

Lucky I took my laptop into the past with me.

Approaching the limit

The mathematical study of time is linked to motion as well as geometry, especially the speed of light. Advanced theories show that as objects get faster and faster—approaching the speed of light—time slows down. Maybe one day calculations in this area really will lead to time travel.

RUSSIA HAS NINE TIME ZONES. THE SUN CAN BE RISING IN THE EAST JUST AS IT'S SETTING IN THE WEST.

Time travel today

Of course, you could say that time travel is already possible. Time and space are linked right across the Earth. If it's noon on one side of the planet, it's midnight on the other. Those places will always be 12 hours apart. We divide the Earth north-south into 24 time zones. Each is one hour ahead of, or behind, its neighbors. One of those divisions even divides today from tomorrow. A fast plane flies faster than the time zones. So if you are on a jet flying west, you could land before you take off. You are a time traveler!

One day, might we turn up at an airport for a journey back in time?

125

abacus A type of counting frame with beads that slide along rods.

Arabic numerals The number symbols 0, 1, 2, 3 etc. that we use today.

area The space inside 2-dimensional objects.

axis An imaginary line around which an object rotates.

base The numbers that are used in a counting system. For example, base 10 uses numbers 0 to 9, base 2 (the binary system) uses only two numbers, 0 and 1.

binary system The counting system that uses only two numbers, 0 and 1

bit In computers, the smallest unit of data (either 0 or 1).

byte A unit of data used by computers, equivalent to 8 bits.

Celsius A temperature scale that uses the freezing point of water as 0 degrees, and the boiling point as 100 degrees.

chaos theory The branch of mathematics that deals with complex systems that are sensitive to tiny changes.

circumference The distance around the edge of a circle.

commutative In math, an operation where it makes no difference if the order of the numbers is changed around.

constellation A group of stars that seem to form a pattern in the sky when we view them from Earth.

decimal place In the decimal system, the position of a number in relation to the decimal point which determines its value.

decimal system The system of counting that uses base 10—multiples of 10.

density The weight of an object compared to the amount of space it fills.

diameter The distance of a straight line from side to side passing through the center of a circle.

digit Any of the numbers 0 to 9.

equation A mathematical statement that says that two things are equal. It will have an equals sign (=) in the middle.

equilateral An object with all of its sides the same length.

exponent A number says how many times to use that number in a multiplication. It is written as a small number to the right and above the base number.

exponential growth Growth of a system in proportion to its size—so the bigger the number the bigger the growth.

Fahrenheit A temperature scale that uses a zero that is 32 degrees colder than the freezing point of water.

Fibonacci sequence The number sequence 0, 1, 1, 2, 3, 5, 8 etc. in which each number is the sum of the previous two numbers.

fraction Part of a whole.

geometry The branch of math that deals with points, lines, shapes, and angles.

gigabyte A unit of data used by computers, equivalent to 1,073,741,824 bytes.

GPS (Global Positioning System) A system that uses information from satellites to work out your position on Earth.

gravity The force that attracts bodies toward the center of the Earth.

hexagon A six-sided shape.

inch A unit of length. There are 12 inches in a foot.

infinity Something that goes on and on with no bounds or outer edge.

irrational number A number that can't be expressed neatly as a fraction.

Kelvin A temperature scale that starts at absolute zero—the temperature at which all motion stops.
kilobyte A unit of data used by computers, equivalent to 1,000 bytes.

latitude In geography, an imaginary line that shows how far north or south something is.

light-year The distance that light travels in a year.

linear growth Growth of a system by the same amount each time.

longitude In geography, an imaginary line that shows how far east or west something is.

mass A measure of how much matter there is in an object.

meridian A line of longitude.

metric system The decimal measuring system that uses meters, liters, and grammes as units of length, volume, and weight.

number line A line on which numbers are marked at intervals, used to help with simple mathematical operations.

numeral A symbol that stands for a number.

operations In math the things we do to numbers, such as addition, subtraction, multiplication, or division.

pentagon A five-sided shape.

perimeter The length around the edge of a shape.

pi The number reached by dividing the circumference of a circle by its diameter (approximately 3.14). It is a constant, or unchanging, number.

prime meridian The meridian that runs through Greenwich in London, UK, which is 0 degrees longitude.

prime number A number that can only be divided by itself, or one.

probability The branch of mathematics that studies how likely something is to happen.

ratio A way of comparing two numbers of a similar kind.

sphere An object shaped like a ball.

statistics The branch of mathematics that deals with collecting, organizing, and presenting numbers.

symmetry When a shape stays the same whether you flip, slide or turn it.

triangulation A method of working out your position by calculating the differences between sets of information.

volume The space inside 3-dimensional objects.

Index